Teen Dads

Also by Jeanne Warren Lindsay

(Partial listing)

The P.A.R.E.N.T. Approach: How to Teach Young Moms and Dads the Art and Skills of Parenting

Your Baby's First Year

El primer año de tu bebé

The Challenge of Toddlers

El reto de los párvulos

Teen Dads: Rights, Responsibilities and Joys

Teenage Couples — Expectations and Reality

Teenage Couples — Caring, Commitment and Change

Teenage Couples — Coping with Reality

Pregnant? Adoption Is an Option

Do I Have a Daddy? A Story for a Single-Parent Child

By Jeanne Lindsay and Jean Brunelli

Your Pregnancy and Newborn Journey

Tu embarazo y el nacimiento de tu bebé

Nurturing Your Newborn: Young Parents' Guide to Baby's First Month

Crianza del recién nacido

By Jeanne Lindsay and Sally McCullough

Discipline from Birth to Three

La disciplina hasta los tres años

By Jeanne Lindsay, Jean Brunelli, and Sally McCullough

Mommy, I'm Hungry!

¡Mami, tengo hambre!

Teen Dads

Rights, Responsibilities, and Joys

Jeanne Warren Lindsay, MA

Buena Park, California

Teen Dads: Rights, Responsibilities and Joys
is part of a seven-book series. Other series titles are:
Your Pregnancy and Newborn Journey
Spanish - ***Tu embarazo y el nacimiento de tu bebé***
Nurturing Your Newborn
Spanish - ***Crianza del recién nacido***
Mommy, I'm Hungry!
Spanish - ***¡Mami, tengo hambre!***
Your Baby's First Year
Spanish - ***El primer año de tu bebé***
The Challenge of Toddlers
Spanish - ***El reto de los párvulos***
Discipline from Birth to Three
Spanish - ***La disciplina hasta los tres años***
Note: The "regular" editions of the above titles are written at sixth grade reading level.
Your Pregnancy and Newborn Journey, Nurturing Your Newborn, Your Baby's First Year, and ***Discipline from Birth to Three*** are also available in easier reading editions which test GL 2 using the Flesch Grade Level Formula.

Library of Congress Cataloging-in-Publication data available upon request.

ISBN 978-1-932538-86-1

MORNING GLORY PRESS, INC.
6595 San Haroldo Way Buena Park, CA 90620-3748
714.828.1998 1.888.612.8254
e-mail jwl@morningglorypress@aol.com
Website www.morningglorypress.com
Printed and bound in the United States of America

CONTENTS

PREFACE

If you are or soon will be a teenage father, you probably hope to be involved in your child's life. Many teen fathers have told me how much they want their child to have a father, to know him, spend time with him. Many of these young dads grew up without a close relationship with their fathers. They want something different for their children.

Even if you want to be with your child, you may already be facing difficulties. Perhaps you aren't with your baby's mother any longer. Or maybe her parents don't want her to see you.

Many young fathers (and mothers) don't know a lot about caring for a baby or an older child. You might feel awkward as you diaper your baby, and you might even find Mom laughing at your efforts. If this happens to you, encourage her to show you how.

If you don't live with your baby, how can you relate to

your son or daughter? On the other hand, you may be very involved in your child's life. You and his/her mother may be living together, or married. Some single teen fathers have custody of their child.

This book is written for all young fathers who want to parent their child(ren) well. You'll hear from other young dads who share their stories and their fatherhood tips. In fact, 64 teenage fathers were interviewed for this book and are quoted here. They are the most important part of the book.

As each young father is quoted, he is identified by his age and the age of his child(ren) and the child(ren)'s mother. If the same person is quoted again in the same chapter, only his name is listed. Names have been changed, but the quotes and the ages given are always real.

Teen Dads covers the parenting basics. If you want more detailed guidance, see the Teens Parenting series of books. ***Your Pregnancy and Newborn Journey, Nurturing Your Newborn, Mommy, I'm Hungry!, Your Baby's First Year, The Challenge of Toddlers,*** and ***Discipline from Birth to Three*** are written directly to teenage parents.

If you are a teenage father, you probably love your child dearly. You'd like to be the best possible parent. You also want to deal with such issues as your relationship with your child's mother and her family and planning for your future. ***Teen Dads*** is written especially to help you meet your goals in parenting — to be a good father and to live the most satisfying life possible.

Best wishes and good luck!

Jeanne Lindsay
May, 2008

FOREWORD

In my opinion, most teen fathers get a bad rap. My experience with many young fathers has shown me they have a genuine desire to be good parents. However, their youth gets in the way. Also, the lack of older male role models in their lives may set the tone for how involved they are and will become. The absence of the older, positive male role model leaves a young father lacking the resources he needs to tune into the role of parent. Without these resources, chances are his struggle will be greater. Compound this struggle with his possible involvement with the Juvenile Justice System, and you have added another set of issues confronting some young parents.

Fortunately, in the past fifteen years national attention has focused on male involvement in pregnancy prevention and parenting. In 1995, President Clinton launched a government-wide initiative to strengthen the role of fathers in families.

There has also been a demand for communities to develop proposals to attract Federal funding for programs on male involvement. In 1997, the California Wellness Foundation funded a guide, *Involving Males in Preventing Teen Pregnancy*. Written by The Urban Institute, the report describes 25 male involvement programs nationwide, all involving males in teenage pregnancy prevention programs. The guide also uses data from the National Survey of Adolescent Males (NSAM) to draw a national picture of young men's risk for causing unplanned pregnancy, and highlighting opportunities for influencing their behavior.

A program highlighted in this guide is the Teen Parenting Skills Project at the Bernalillo County Juvenile Detention Center, Albuquerque, New Mexico. The project works with incarcerated teenage mothers and fathers, pregnant and parenting. The project focuses on providing a venue for teenage parents to come together as a group and share basic educational information about parenting; provide a referral source for community-based agencies; and address issues regarding long distance communication for those going into the adult system. The resident population at the Detention Center normally runs 90 percent male. With this in mind, the program takes on a strong male involvement emphasis in its programming.

The project offers basic education in parenting skills, and deals with family dynamics, the birthing process, developmental milestones, child abuse/domestic violence issues, newborn care, male involvement, infant massage, job skills, anger management, car seat safety, fetal alcohol syndrome, and other issues. Different classes have been provided as community agencies have requested or been asked to share information on their programs.

The teen parenting project sessions include a great deal of time addressing the incarceration time away from parenting. Participation in the project is on a volunteer basis, and those who participate are eligible for a one-hour visit with their significant other and child once a week. A great deal of time is also spent discussing breaking the negative cycles so often associated with very early parenting. For example, the teen sons of adolescent mothers are 2.7 times more likely to land in prison than the sons of mothers who delayed childbirth until their early twenties, according to *Kids Having Kids*. (Robin Hood Foundation).

A program in New Mexico which addresses teen fathers and their need for resources is the New Mexico Young Fathers Project. It began in the summer of 1999 as a pilot project using older male mentors to provide services in the facility and in the community. The project is funded through the New Mexico Department of Health and administered by the New Mexico Teen Pregnancy Coalition. The project runs a weekly group in the Detention Center. Mentors from the project also visit the teen fathers individually throughout the week.

The project offers assistance in job hunting, educational placement, and weekly groups in the community. The project has also moved its program into several correctional facilities surrounding the Detention Center, where those young fathers moving into another system can still meet and discuss parenting issues.

Part of the Teen Parenting Skills Project is to hand out educational resources that could be of benefit to these young parents. With the help of some funding, the project gives away copies of *Teen Dads: Rights, Responsibilities and Joys*. The teens, male and female, enjoy the information and share this with their significant others at visitation. Basic issues of parenting are discussed in *Teen Dads*, and provide a background for group discussions.

Gang involvement is one of the issues we discuss with adolescents incarcerated in the Juvenile Detention Center. It is my strong opinion that gang involvement gets in the way of parenting — it's a bad mix, as witnessed by young fathers consistently returning to the facility with a more serious charge than before. These new charges can eventually place them further into the system, and more often than not, moves them into the adult system. This means more time away from their child and leaves their partner parenting on her own.

I appreciate Jeanne Warren Lindsay and Morning Glory Press for their various publications, especially *Teen Dads* and *Discipline from Birth to Three*. These books have been extremely helpful in providing information to these young parents, and in getting many a discussion started.

Robert Estevan Pacheco
Project Facilitator/Program Manager
Bernalillo County Juvenile Detention Center
Albuquerque, New Mexico

ACKNOWLEDGMENTS

I'm most grateful to the 64 young fathers I interviewed especially for this book and to other young men who have contributed their expertise. Some gave me permission to thank them by name. They include those interviewed specifically for this edition of ***Teen Dads:*** Margarito Alfaro, Frederick Cervantes, Jesus Gonzales, George Guillen, Jeff Huff, Jonathan Lopez, Jose Tinajero, Robert Valencia, Irving Olvera, Jaime Ramirez, Jr., and John Sturgeon, Jr.

I have also interviewed Patrick Candelaria, Brian Heppler, Clifton Montoya, Joseph Bustamonte, Victor Garcia, Edvardo Alcaraz, Sean Christian, Renell Simmons, Gerardo Ortega, Victor Sarduy, Christopher Medaglia, Matthew Flannelly, Matthew Topchi, Jose Sanchez, Mizraim Leal, Chris Rismiller, Albert Aguilar, Ryan Hollmann, Jason Kucharek, Harry Lyles, Ruben Nora, Richard L. Ellison, Edgar Alcala, Frank Villalobos, Herman Hernandez, Chris Mitchell, Dana Broshar, John Bernardino, Sam Thompson, Gary Gracely, Jr., Jason Brinckman, Eddie Escobar, Carl Miller, Jason Taylor, Sam Vasquez, Rob Blackmon, Chris Focht, An Nguyen, and Ray Ramirez.

Sharon Iriye, Bob Malehorn, Lisa Sadowsky, Barry McIntosh, Rita Vogel, Nancy Nicolisi, Lisa Montoya, Robert Pacheco, Lynn Coleman, Julie Vetica, Pat Alviso, David Crawford, Kenneth Easum, Annette Cooper, Peggy McNabb, Barbara Kolar, Pat Clark, Teresa Branham, Steve Burkhard, Paula Cross, Sheila Konfino, and Chris Dwyer referred clients for interviewing and/or provided other help. Their assistance was invaluable.

For this edition, I also interviewed Barry McIntosh, parent educator, New Mexico Young Fathers Project; Carlos Balladares, bilingual case manager, NMYFP; Jesus Gonzales, former case manager, NMYEP; Mara Duncan, teacher, West County Detention Facility, Richmond, California; Darryl Green, Male Services Facilitator, Casey Family Services, Baltimore, Maryland; and Judy Bauerle, retired health educator, former leader of Read to Me Program for incarcerated parents. I appreciate the wisdom each of these people shared with me.

Angela Allen-Hess, teacher in the Teen Parent Program, Paramount, California, supplied most of the photographs. Her models were her wonderful students. Some of the photos were provided by the late David Cawford, Teen Parent teacher, Sacramento, California.

Jean Brunelli, PHN, reviewed the manuscript and offered helpful suggestions.

Tim Rinker is the cover artist. I continue to appreciate his creativity.

I am extremely grateful for the contributions of all of these talented people.

Eve Wright again helped with the proof-reading and kept Morning Glory Press alive and well during book production time. I thank her for her valuable support.

Most of all, I appreciate Bob (now deceased), the wonderful father of our five children, and my love for half a century.

Jeanne Lindsay

To the young fathers
who share their wisdom
and their love for their children
so freely on these pages

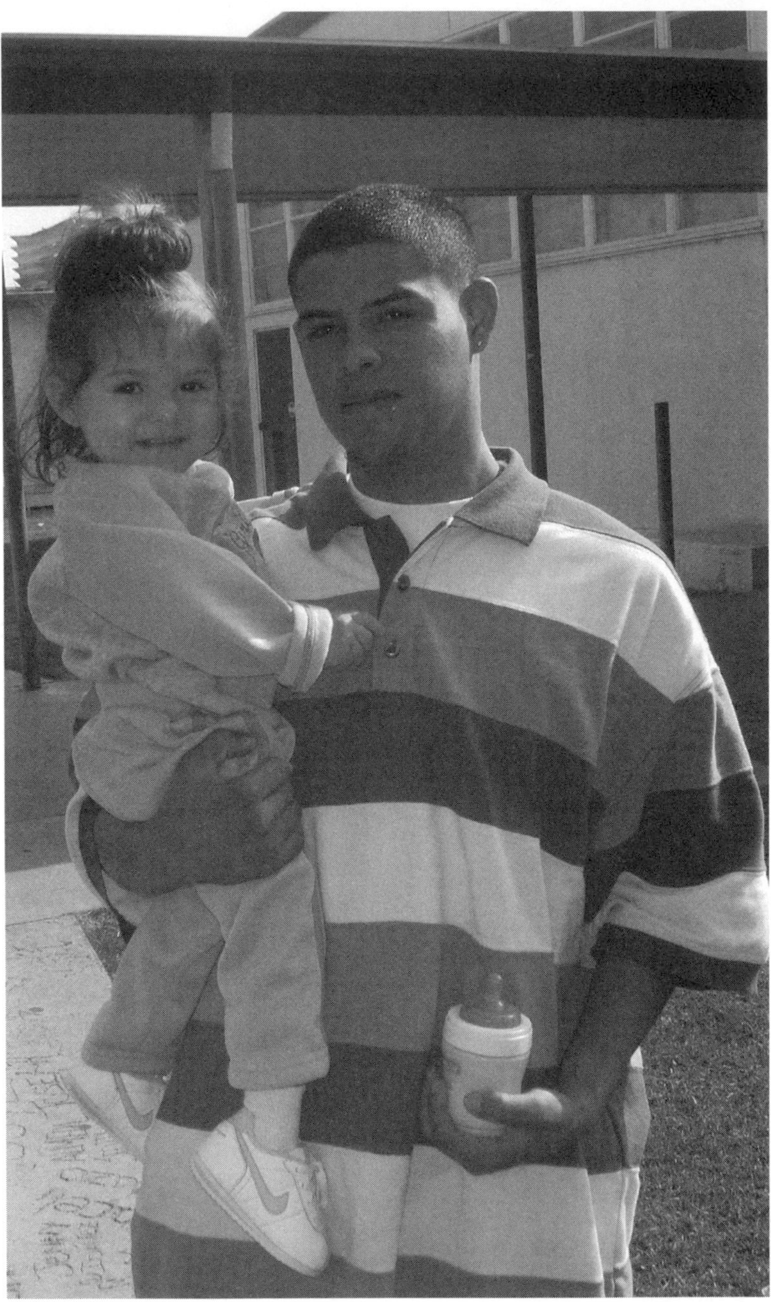

"A good father is someone who's there for his kids." (Danny)

1

Especially for Dad

- **If you don't live with your baby**
- **If you and Mom aren't together**
- **Establishing paternity**
- **It's not easy**

The hard thing is you're still a kid. You can't deny it. You got yourself into this mess.

I wish I had never had kids. There are a lot of things I'd like to be doing now, but I can't change what I've done. I have to deal with it even though sometimes I say, "This sucks." I see my friends who don't have kids, and I wish I were like them.

Now I have to think about my baby when I'm walking on the street. It feels weird. Before, I didn't have anyone to think about except me. Now I have to watch out for all three of us. I was mostly raised to take care of myself. I understood there wouldn't be anybody there to help me out.

Now I have to think of them. It's hard.

Andy, 17 - Gus, 5 months (Yolanda, 15)

A good father is someone who's there for his kids, there to teach them, care for them, love them, show them how to get through life. I want to be a good dad.

Danny, 18 - Ashley, 15 months; Aaron, 3 weeks (Disiree, 16)

If you're a teen father — or will be soon — what about you? People say teen fathers don't care about their babies. They only want to make girls pregnant. They say teenage fathers forget about their children and their children's mothers.

Some teen fathers don't get involved. Some may seem not to care about their children. But you probably aren't like that. If you were, you wouldn't be reading this book.

Perhaps you live with your baby's mother. You may be married, although less than one in five teenage mothers is married when her baby is born.

If You Don't Live with Your Baby

You may have a close relationship with your baby's mother even if you're not living together. Perhaps you took prepared childbirth classes together. You may have been deeply involved coaching the mother throughout labor and delivery. Perhaps you're caring for the baby as much as you can.

If the baby's parents are not married, how much "should" the father be included? If the young family lives together, they probably feel much the same about joint parenting as do married couples. If they don't live together, there is no pattern cut and ready for them to follow.

Many fathers who don't live with their children want a

strong relationship with them. Miguel is an example. He lived with his daughter's mother for several months after Genevieve was born. In fact, if he had his way, he would still be living with his family. Since that's impossible, he spends as much time with Genevieve as he can:

I'll continue to keep Genevieve whenever I can and buy her things she needs. Today I didn't go to work so I kept Genny all day. She's not only my daughter — she's like a little friend. I was playing with her all day. She's all active — she gets me tired, but I love her so much I'd do anything for her. She goes in all the rooms, and I have to be alert.

She's smart. She does things I wouldn't think she would do. I'll tell her to go get me a diaper. She'll do it, and I'll give her a hug. Every time she does something good, I hug her.

Miguel, 20 - Genevieve, 18 months (Maurine, 16)

If You and Mom Aren't Together

I think fathers mainly split because they're scared. If you aren't with your baby's mom you can still play a role in your child's life. If you and the mom don't get along, it doesn't mean you can't see your baby.

Tiger, 19 - Chanté, 18 months (Crystal, 18)

If you aren't with your baby's mother, you can still have a relationship with your child. Unless the court forbids it, you have a right to see your child and to spend time with him. If you aren't able to provide for him financially at this point, share your time.

In some states, visitation is tied to providing child support, but this is not the case in most states. The father usually has the right to see his child whether or not he's paying support.

Legally, he may be able to have his child part of the

time. Some fathers have custody of their children. Parents who don't agree should talk to a lawyer or legal aid group.

Establishing Paternity

I don't want to be like my father so I'll be establishing paternity at the end of this month. I want to stay in contact with my son, do things with him.

Lester, 17 - Shaquille, 16 months (Traci, 16)

If you and your baby's mother are not married, it's important that you establish paternity. This means you both sign legal papers stating you are the father of your child. If you don't, your child might not be able to claim Social Security, insurance benefits, veterans' and other types of benefits through you. This is also the only legal way for an unmarried father to establish his right to visitation or custody. Usually the easiest way to claim peternity is to sign the form after delivery while your partner and baby are still in the hospital.

When you visit your child, keep a record of the visits. Get written receipts for the money you provide for child support. You'll need these written records if you go to court. Incidentally, try not to make verbal threats to baby's mother. Making threats could be held against you in court which might lead to you being denied visitation rights. Besides, your baby will be ahead if you and his mother, even if you aren't together, can put your differences aside when you're talking about your child.

Your child needs you. If you aren't through school yet, you may not be able to pay your share of his support. Instead, this is the time to obtain job skills so that you'll be able soon to pay for at least half of your child's needs.

You don't need to wait until you're older to give your child your love, caring, and emotional support. Even if you can't pay all the bills at this point, you can be supportive in many other ways. That's what this book is all about.

I didn't consider leaving because my father did that to my mother. You could say I hate him for what he did to my mother, and I don't want to do that. I grew up hating him because he wasn't there for me. Why would I want to ruin my kid's life by doing that?

Last time I saw my father was when I was five years old. I have a pretty bad picture of him. We saw him on the sidewalk, and I said "Hi." He ignored me.

Jacob, 19 - Sophie, 7 months (Lynette, 18)

It's Not Easy

Many young fathers discussed the difficulties of having a child before they were ready. Of course it's hard. Parenting a child is one of the hardest — and one of the most rewarding — tasks faced by human beings. Getting pregnant before she's ready changes a young woman's life.

It also changes your life. Many teen fathers choose to support and share in their child's care. They do so even though they may face hardship and broken dreams just as their baby's mother does. They know how important a father's influence is on his son or daughter.

Having a baby changed my life a lot. I had to stop doing about everything, going to parties, hanging out. I had to focus on Jaysay, meeting his needs. I have to be mature and stand up for whatever he needs, be a man because I've responsibilities now.

Darrance, 17 - Jaysay, 1 year (Victoria, 17)

When you choose this route, you will see your baby grow. First, you'll see her become a charming and independent toddler. You can be there as she travels through childhood. Finally, you can see her become a responsible, mature adult.

What a wonderful opportunity.

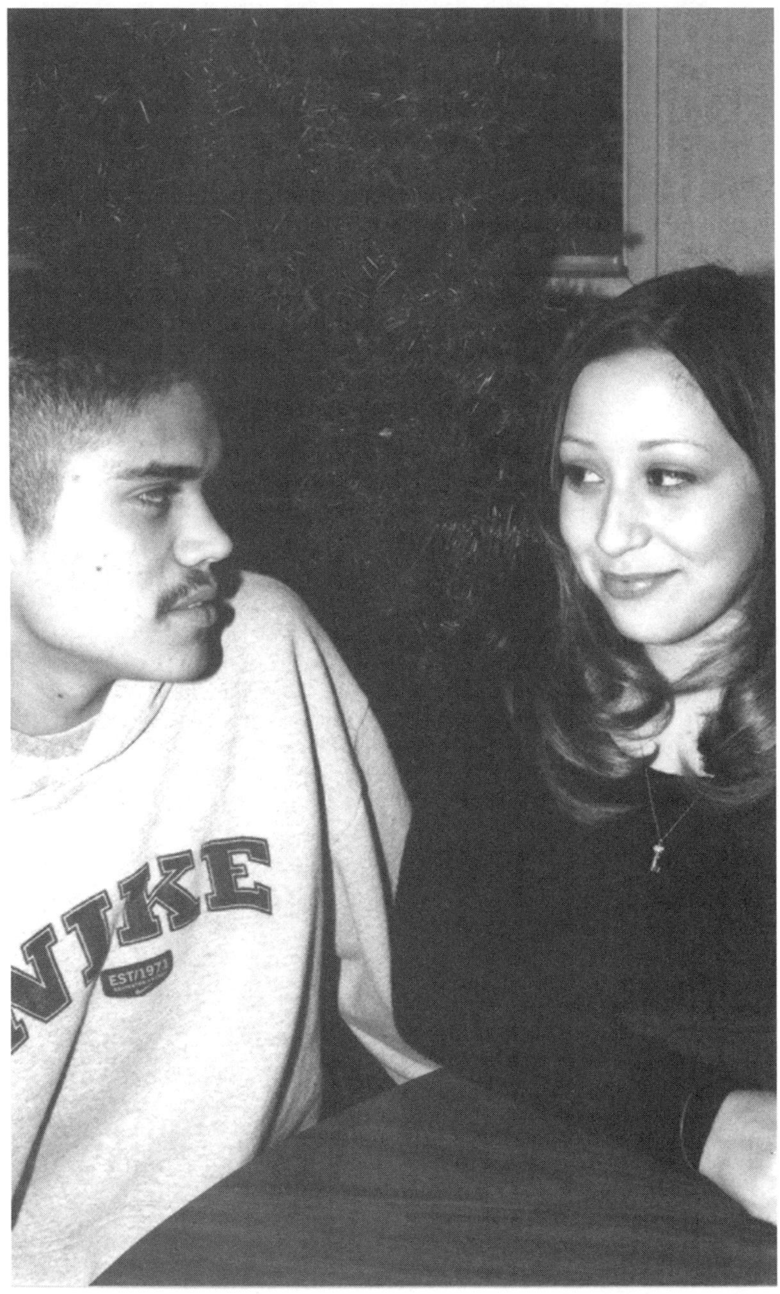

"What would you do if we had a kid?" (Marc)

2

Is She Pregnant?

- Early pregnancy test is vital
- How do you feel about this pregnancy?
- Her parents may reject you
- Don't drop out!
- Importance of school for Mom
- Adoption is still an option
- Father's rights in adoption
- Your emotional support is vital

It was a shock to me. I didn't want to be a father. I was too young. I thought we was just playing around. Then all at once Trudy came up with something real serious. She lived around the block from me, and I tried to avoid her.

I ran away from it for awhile. Then I went back to Trudy. My dad left when I was born. I didn't want that for my baby.

Trudy was moody, always snapping. She was scared, too, but she didn't pressure me. I kept telling her I wasn't going to leave her.

I wasn't with her in the hospital. That was because her dad don't like me. I didn't see Nathan until he was a week old.

I used to hang out on the streets while Trudy was pregnant. After Nathan was born I changed. When I saw my kid, how he looked like me, I calmed down.

I quit school because we didn't have any money. I got a job. Then I started back to school last fall. Next month I'm going back on Independent Study. We need more money, so I have to go back to work.

Esteban, 18 - Nathan, 2; Ralph, 5 months (Trudy, 17)

When Melinda told me she was pregnant, I didn't come home. I went out to a friend's house and got plastered. I said, "Well, she's been asking me for awhile, saying 'What would you do if we had a kid?'"

I was overwhelmed. I was living with my father, and he kicked me out. He said, "You've got to take responsibility, you've got to get a job and go take care of her." So I went to live with her. It's working out okay.

Marc, 16 - Koary, 14 months (Melinda, 18)

Early Pregnancy Test Is Vital

I went to the doctor with her for the ultrasound, and for the first pregnancy test. We did a home test and it came out positive, but we wanted to check for sure so we went to the hospital for a blood test.

We found out he was a boy with the ultrasound.

Todd, 18 - Avery, 6 months (Celia, 19)

Do you and your partner think she might be pregnant but aren't sure? Please help her see a doctor. Getting an early pregnancy test is important for several reasons:

- She might not be pregnant. If she isn't, and you and she

don't want her to be pregnant, you have two choices: Don't have sex. If you do, use birth control.

- She has more choices early in her pregnancy. She could choose to have an abortion. An abortion is safer and easier for the woman if it's done during the first twelve weeks of pregnancy. She has the legal right to decide for or against abortion whether or not you agree.

I really wasn't that happy about the pregnancy. I tried to persuade her to get an abortion but she didn't want that. I kept pressing it until she'd say, "Okay, okay," just to shut me up. But she didn't do it.

If you're old enough to have sex, you have to be able to deal with the responsibilities that come from it. The father has no choice in what the girl wants to do. It's her choice because she's the one carrying the baby. I didn't have no choice, but I let her know what might happen also.

I thought I was too young. Being a father would screw up my life. Now that I have Katie, I'm happy.

Ryan, 17 - Katie, 7 weeks (Jennifer, 18)

- She needs to see the doctor if she's continuing her pregnancy. The doctor will help her care for the unborn baby so it will be born healthy.

- Some couples choose to release the baby for adoption. Adoption planning is best done fairly early in the pregnancy although the final decision cannot be made until after the baby is born.

Important as prenatal care is, doctors cost a lot. Do you have health insurance through your work? Or can she get prenatal care through her family's health plan? If not, can she get Medicaid? Call your local Department of Public Social Services (Welfare Department) to find out.

Some areas have prenatal health clinics. Women can get

prenatal check-ups for no charge, or they may be charged according to their income.

How Do *You* Feel About This Pregnancy?

First I was in shock. I didn't know what to do. I guess I was in denial, but in the back of my head I knew it was true.

After that I felt, I don't know, nice, that I'm going to have my own kid, my own blood. Before I found out Lynette was pregnant, I wasn't doing anything. But when I found out, I got a job right away.

Jacob, 19 - Sophie, 7 months (Lynette, 18)

Learning his partner is pregnant makes some teenage fathers happy. At the same time, they may feel scared as they think of the responsibilities they're facing.

I was scared when she told me she was pregnant. I was working, but I didn't know how I was going to support her and the baby. I couldn't even support myself. I was also real excited. I was happy, but I was scared.

I knew everything was going to be different. Nothing would ever be the same again. I felt like my freedom was going to be taken away. I couldn't come and go as I pleased, but I wanted to do the right thing. I wanted my daughter to have a father.

Carlos, 19 - Elena, 23 months (Monica, 18)

Your child needs your love and care. He also needs your financial support. Both parents are required by law to support their child.

Her Parents May Reject You

I had problems with her mom, and we were always hostile. I really didn't like her, and she didn't like me.

She had Aracely at 17, and she didn't want the same thing for Aracely.

Sergio, 17 - Yvette, 11 months (Aracely, 17)

Your partner's parents may not want you around. Their daughter is no longer a carefree teenager. She is now or soon will be a hardworking mother, and they may blame you.

Her parents and I were pretty close. When they learned Darlene was pregnant, they had anger for me. I wasn't wanted in their house. Now that the baby is born, they're pretty happy. They like me again.

It really puts you down when they reject you. That's what they were doing. I stuck in there because in my heart I wanted to be with my child.

I would say to Darlene, "I understand why they feel like that, but why don't they give us a chance?"

Manuel, 18 - Juan, 27 months; Darcy, 13 months (Darlene, 18)

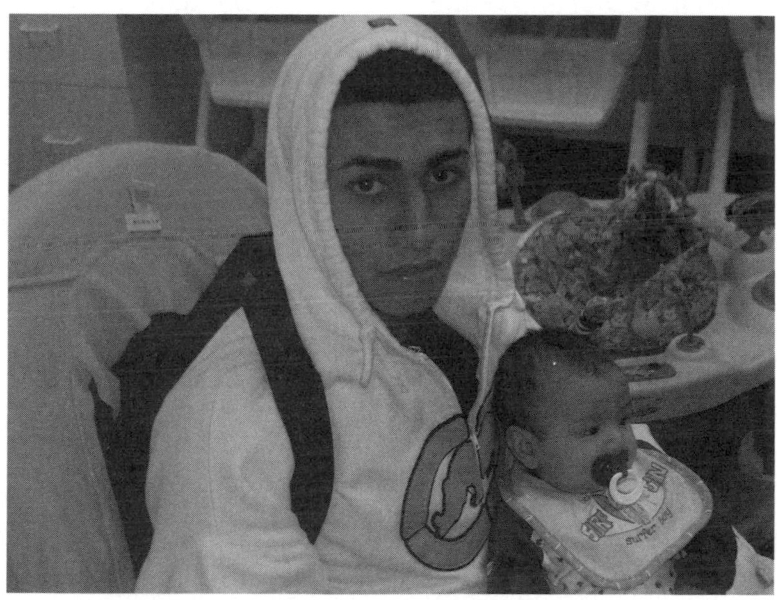

Am I ready for a baby?

If you have this problem with your partner's parents, perhaps you can convince them you're their grandchild's father, and that you want to do your best to parent your child well. They may realize that you are, indeed, a positive influence on this grandchild they probably adore.

It will work. When her dad used to get mad at me and tell me to get out of this place, I'd leave. Then I'd come back the next day, and we would settle our problems. The more we talk and the more we get closer, the better it will be.

Alvaro, 17 (Sophia, 17 - 6 months pregnant)

Don't Drop Out!

Jocelyn wrote a letter to me at school telling me she was scared because she hadn't had her period. At first, I freaked out. I was really scared. I didn't know how to be a father. I only needed one more credit to graduate, but everything happened so quick, how am I going to take care of a baby without money? I dropped out and got a job.

Tim, 20 - Chamique, 21 months (Jocelyn, 19)

Some young men drop out of school when they learn their partner is pregnant. They feel they must get a job and support their family.

Is this how you feel? It's a hard decision. If you drop out of school, you probably won't get a well-paying job. Without even a high school diploma, you may never be able to support your family as you'd like. If you must go to work full-time, you should enroll in your school's Independent or Work Study program.

Most young people need good career counseling. Perhaps your school can tell you about job training. Intensive job training now can help you get a job with a future.

Fathers and mothers who continue their education and

hold good jobs obviously are much better off than are par-ents who quit school and must take whatever low-paying job they can find.

> *First I want to get my GED* (General Equivalency Diploma) *and start moving on, then train with computers. I worry about the future a little. I don't want to be real old and still making minimum wage. I want to be financially secure.*
>
> Miguel, 20 - Genevieve, 18 months (Maurine, 16)

Shaun was enrolled in college when he learned he'd be a father soon. With help from his parents, he's staying in school. He says this is the best thing he can do now:

> *I was shocked at the pregnancy test. I cried with her. For a couple of weeks you can't think. I was in college and knew I wanted to stay there. I'd have a baby to take care of. I had to get through college. I hoped my parents would understand and help me, and they have.*
>
> *If I didn't stay in school, I couldn't get a good job. I could work at some job with no future. I'd rather struggle the next couple of years. That's better than struggling for the rest of our lives.*
>
> Shaun, 19 - Troy, 2 months (Bethann, 17)

Importance of School for Mom

> *I was very upset that she quit going to school. I'd like her out of school as soon as possible. Her high school diploma is very important, and she agrees.*
>
> Shaun

Is your partner in school? If she hasn't graduated, it's important that she continue her education. She, like you, needs an education and job skills.

It's not legal for public schools to push students out of

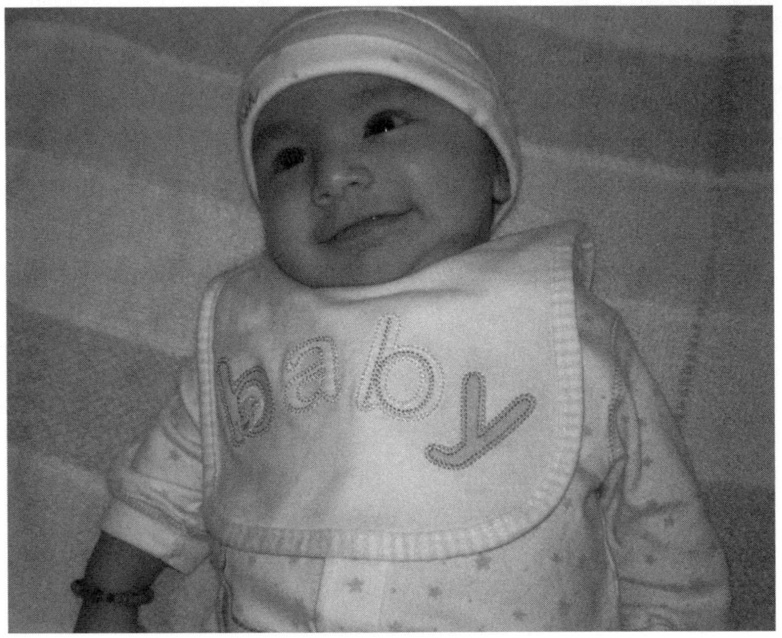

She'd like both parents to learn the art and skills of parenting.

school because of pregnancy or because they're married. However, she might prefer a special program for school-age parents. Ask the school counselor if there is such a program in her school district. If she chooses a special program, she can take prenatal health and parenting classes. She can also get help in solving problems caused by her pregnancy.

If you're a student at the school, you should be able to enroll in the special class with her. In fact, if your school has a parenting class, you should be welcome whether or not your baby's mother is a student there.

When I knew Donia was pregnant I felt I needed to get involved. I looked for help anywhere I could get it. I talked to some people in the Teen Parent Program at our school, and they told me I might be the only guy.

I enrolled. I saw that as a good opportunity to set

an example for more teen dads to go to the program where they can really get help.

Emilio, 17 - Alejandro, 3 weeks (Donia, 15)

To find this kind of help, check with a school counselor. If there is no help there, talk to a social worker, or you might find a program for teen dads through a local church or synagogue.

Jocelyn was in the teen parent class at school and I was with Bob (counseling program). It was a group of five or six guys. Even though I dropped out, I would still go to school for the group.

In the group, Bob would talk about what a father should do and should not do. Mostly he was there to help us with anything we needed — get us on WIC, clothes for the baby, other resources.

Tim

Adoption Is Still an Option

Most pregnant teens either have an abortion or they continue their pregnancy and parent their child themselves. There is another option, however — adoption.

A generation or two ago, some unmarried pregnant teens decided to let another family parent their child. They never expected to see their child again. This was called closed adoption. This was extremely hard for the birthparents.

Adoption has changed. Today, pregnant women and their partners considering adoption may choose the people who will parent their child. They may meet these people. Together, they may agree that the birthparents may see their child occasionally. They may exchange letters and pictures throughout the years. This is called open adoption.

During pregnancy, you and your partner need to make a plan. For many, this is a parenting plan. For others, it is an adoption plan. Either way, you plan for your child's future.

Father's Rights in Adoption

Adoption laws vary from one state to another. In Canada, each province has different adoption laws.

The birthmother must sign the adoption papers. The birthfather generally must also sign them.

Usually, the adoption can proceed if the father signs *one* of these papers:

Father's Legal Options

1. He gives permission for the adoption.
2. He denies he is the father.
3. He gives up his rights to the child.

What if your partner decides on adoption and you decide not to sign anything? State laws vary. If you don't sign, the adoption may take longer or it may not happen.

Your Emotional Support Is Vital

Your emotional support is important to your partner. It's probably the most important thing you can offer right now.

Most women are easily upset during pregnancy. This is caused by hormonal changes. It doesn't matter if the pregnancy is planned or not. Whatever her age, these hormonal changes are very real. If she seems crabby, be patient.

Your partner may have other problems. Her parents may be upset about the pregnancy. It's hard for her to continue her education. The future may look pretty scary. Your support can help her deal with these feelings.

You also may feel a lot of pressure and confusion about your situation. Try talking to a knowledgable adult you trust. This may help.

Justin and Janel decided not to tell anyone about their pregnancy until the last minute. Janel didn't even tell her best friend. This was very hard on her because she felt she needed her friend's support:

Janel wanted somebody to talk to, and sometimes she'd just break down and say, "I can't do it. I have to tell somebody." But I convinced her. I'd say, "Hey, listen, it's only a month or two away. and your dad'll either kill me or beat me up if we tell him now." She didn't want that.

Justin, 20 - Niele, 2; Alan, 3 months (Janel, 19)

When they finally told her parents, not long before their baby was born, both sets of parents were surprisingly accepting. It would have been much better for Janel (and for Justin) to have shared their news far earlier and gotten the help they needed.

The fact that you're reading this book means you're taking the steps necessary to help make things better. The next chapter suggests ways you can be involved in parenting your child long before he is born.

When you're there during pregnancy, you're getting an early start on parenting.

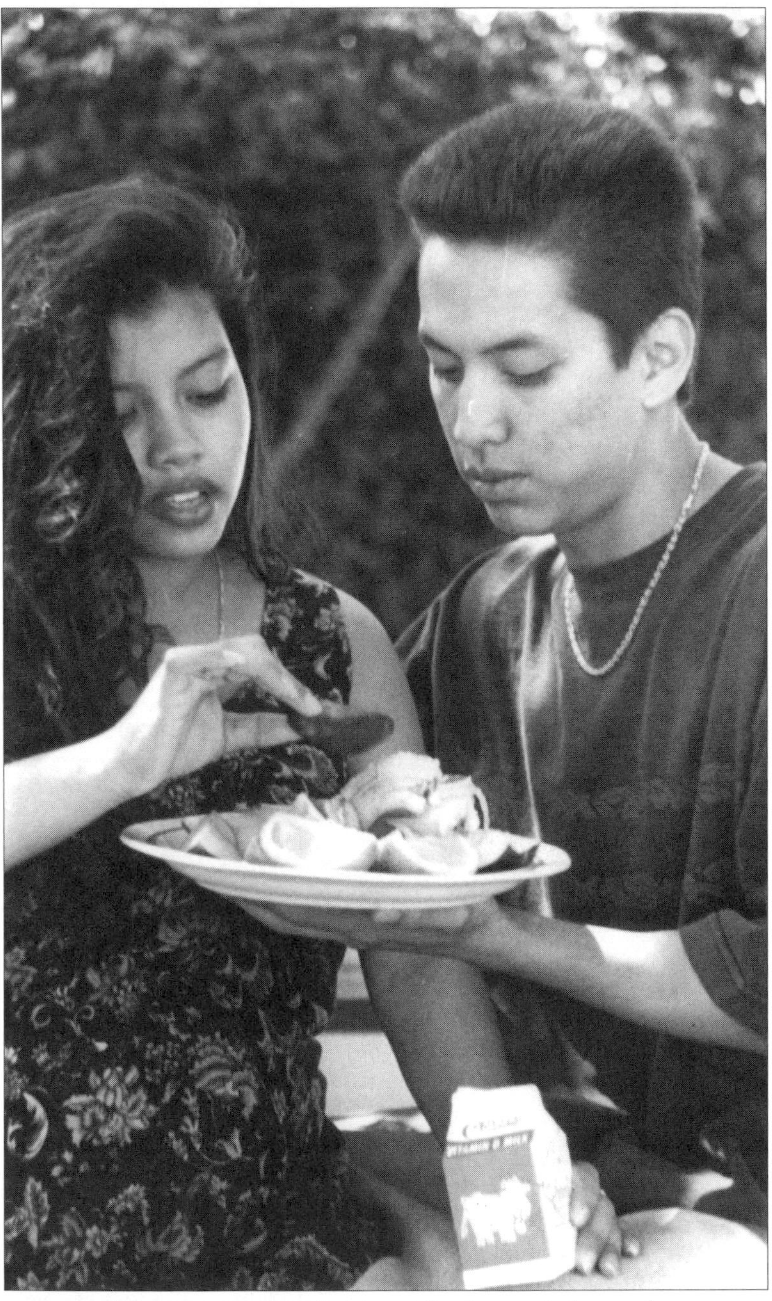

You can encourage her to eat foods your baby needs.

3

Parenting Starts With Pregnancy

- **Checking on your baby**
- **Is she moody?**
- **She may not feel well**
- **Help for discomforts**
- **Sharing your time**
- **What she eats matters**
- **Limiting the fat**
- **The fast food dilemma**
- **Smoking harms fetus**
- **Drugs and pregnancy**
- **Fetal alcohol syndrome (FAS)**
- **Bonding with baby**
- **Baby feels crowded**
- **You have an important task**

My life changed a lot during pregnancy. We stopped going out so much and mostly stayed home.

She had morning sickness 24 hours a day. Once she did feel good, she was gigantic pregnant and had to go to the bathroom all the time. I knew what was going on, and I figured we had to take it day by day.

Greg, 17 - Liana, 1 year (Nicole, 17)

I spent time with her during her pregnancy because the baby was the most important thing to me. Even though you make a mistake, you can't call a baby a mistake because it's the most wonderful thing. You have to take care of it as hard as you can.

Khusba, 22 - Merlalcia, 11/2 yr. (Aurora, 17)

Parenting starts with pregnancy. You and your partner can do a lot to help your baby be born healthy and strong.

She should be seeing the doctor at least once a month, and more often during her last trimester. The doctor will probably want to see her each week during her last month.

During Jocelyn's pregnancy I was there for every appointment, every ultrasound. I was there for everything.

Tim, 20 - Chamique, 21 months (Jocelyn, 19)

These visits are extremely important for her and for your baby. If you can go with her, she will probably appreciate your support. You'll feel closer to your child, especially when the doctor lets you listen to his/her heartbeat or you see the ultrasound picture.

Checking on Your Baby

Ultrasound: *A test using sound waves. These waves show the outline of the baby in the uterus.*

Your partner's doctor may talk about an ultrasound. This is done in a doctor's office or at a laboratory.

An ultrasound doesn't hurt at all. It is done to see how baby is growing. It also predicts mom's due date. Certain birth defects can be discovered with an ultrasound. It may tell you whether baby is a boy or girl. (It could be wrong.)

Is she having an ultrasound? If so, ask your doctor for a copy. It's a picture of your baby although it won't look much like a photograph.

Several times during her pregnancy the doctor will have

blood tests done. One will show her blood type. Another is called AFP (alpha feta protein), and it measures the protein in her blood. Many doctors do this test instead of the ultrasound.

Is She Moody?

She's going to act different — she's going to be a lot more moody. You need to understand that, and it's real hard. I don't think I handled it the best.

You need to think about how she's feeling. The biggest thing is they don't feel pretty, and they're scared about the baby being born just like you are.

You're both going through a lot of pressure. You're still young, too, but you need to take responsibility. It's the big changing period.

Zach, 19 - Kevin, 20 months (Erica, 16)

Are you finding that your partner is moody and crabby more often than she used to be? The hormones in her body are changing rapidly as the baby develops, and this causes the moodiness. She may also have a lot on her mind, and feel she has too many decisions to make.

She was crabbier during pregnancy. We'd see each other three or four times a week, and we used to get into fights a lot.

The father should just deal with it regardless what mood he's in, just sit there and take it. If she do make you mad, you should walk out and go to the park and relax. Don't turn your back because that puts a big hurt on her.

Jermaine, 18 - Amy, 1 year (Angela, 17)

If you can be patient when she's moody, perhaps be extra thoughtful, she may feel better. Try not to do anything or say anything that will make these moods worse. Continuing depression could have a negative effect on your baby. One thing is sure — she won't be pregnant forever!

She May Not Feel Well

Even though she's seeing her doctor regularly, your partner may not feel well at times. Pregnancy brings changes to a woman's body. Some changes are pleasant, some are unpleasant.

Many women have morning sickness during the first three months. Throwing up each morning is hard to handle. If your partner feels sick, encourage her to drink lukewarm water or herb tea and eat soda crackers. Eating small meals more often may help. She should never use over-the-counter medicine unless her doctor says it's okay.

She's likely to feel tired much of the time. This is because her body is preparing for the baby. You can encourage her to take naps, and you can exercise with her. Taking a walk after lunch or dinner may help as much as a nap.

> *The doctor said it was good for her to walk, so I'd ask her to go for a walk. She'd say, "We have a car. Let's use it."*
>
> *I'd tell her, "We're just going to the corner store." I'd help her up, and we'd walk and talk.*
>
> Alton, 17 - Britney and Jakela, 1 year (Sharrell, 19)

She'll need to go to the bathroom more often, especially during the early part of pregnancy and during the last two or three months before the baby is born.

Your partner's blood supply changes throughout her pregnancy. Her uterus is growing rapidly, which draws more blood to her lower body. She may sometimes feel dizzy, especially if she's been standing for a long time.

If this happens, you can help her lie down with her feet higher than her head. If she can't do that, she should sit down and put her head between her knees, then breathe as deeply as possible.

Help for Discomforts

She may complain of heartburn. If so, she might try eating small meals often, avoid greasy foods, and eat more fruits and vegetables. Doing these things also helps prevent constipation, a common problem during the last weeks of pregnancy.

Her breasts may get bigger and more tender. Her breasts are getting ready to give your baby mother's milk. She may have already noticed the pre-milk, colostrum, leaking from her breasts from time to time. Some moms leak earlier than others, but when they're pregnant, all women's breasts get ready to breastfeed. Did your mother breastfeed you?

This is a good time to talk together about the benefits of breastfeeding your baby. Babies who are breastfed are likely to be healthier than formula-fed infants.

As her pregnancy progresses, her uterus becomes bigger and presses against several organs. These often cause shortness of breath and back problems. Sleeping with extra pillows under her body may help her feel better.

If she exercises throughout pregnancy, she's less likely to have back pain. If her back hurts, heat may make her feel better although she shouldn't sleep on a heating pad.

A back rub can help, so perhaps you can develop your massage skills. If she rests with her legs up, it helps both her back and her legs.

Sharing Your Time

It was difficult. She wanted me there all the time. If I would go to my friends, she'd get mad. I'd try to calm her down. She felt alone, and she was afraid she might have the baby early. I'd talk to her, and she'd understand. If you don't talk to her while she's pregnant, she wonders what's wrong.

Before she got pregnant, I was mostly out with my friends. Then I had to think, I've got to change for the baby. I've got to stop going out — there are too many problems where I live. That changed me a little.

Hugo, 16 - Breanna, 9 months (Marcella, 18)

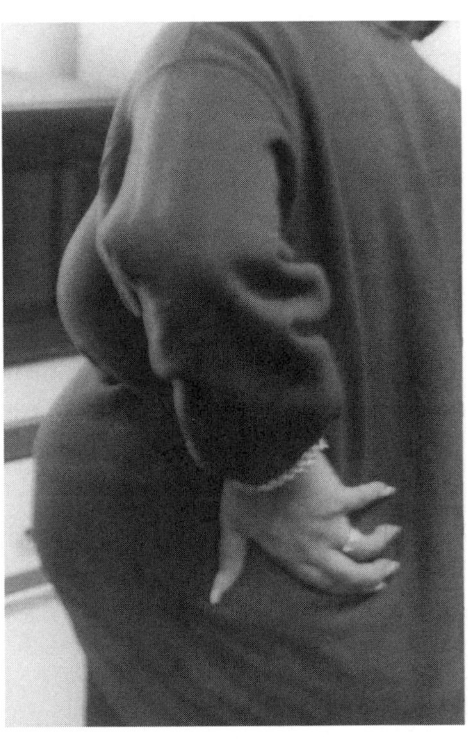

She may feel fat and ugly. Reassure her that pregnancy is also a beautiful time.

She needs your emotional support at this time. She may feel fat and ugly and think you don't care. Reassure her that she's pregnant and pretty. She may need you to spend more *time* with her. This can be far more important than spending money.

She may need to talk with you about the future — your relationship or about parenting the baby. She may be afraid of the future and need your reassurance that she's not alone. Often teen dads are also afraid of what the future will hold but may not be able to admit this to anyone. Talking together may be reassuring to both of you.

Sexual activity is okay unless it hurts her. In the last months of pregnancy, the birth canal becomes shorter, and you may need to find new positions for intercourse. Sexual intercourse should stop if there's any bleeding or her water bag leaks.

Whether or not they're sexually active during pregnancy, many couples feel a special closeness during this time.

What She Eats Matters

Celia had to eat more while she was pregnant. She used to be bulimic, and she's always been a light eater, so we worked on that.

Todd, 18 - Avery, 6 months (Celia, 19)

Encourage her to eat the foods she *and your baby* need.

A mother who does not eat right could have a less than perfect baby, especially if her own body is still growing and maturing. She probably will have a healthy baby if:

- She eats foods she and baby need during pregnancy.
- She stays away from alcohol, cigarettes, and drugs including caffeine.
- She sees her doctor regularly.

You can help her do all these things.

When Bethann was pregnant I'd get on her case. I'd see that she ate right. I would take her to the doctor. I was like a watchdog for her.

Shaun, 19 - Troy, 2 months (Bethann, 17)

If she's like most of us, she won't want to be lectured about her eating habits. If you're together a lot, however, you can be a big influence. The foods she needs to eat now are also good for you. Check out the **<MyPyramid.com>** website. It's an excellent guide to good nutrition.

If you eat foods from each of the groups on **MyPyramid** regularly and go light on the junk food, it will be easier for her to do the same thing. And you'll both feel better.

She also needs to drink 6-8 glasses of water each day.

Water is much better than soda for her and your baby. Too much soda can cause dehydration, which can be serious.

During pregnancy, I made her foods — I'd make dinner for her. I'd chop up fruit and tell her to eat healthy foods.

It changed my diet too — I was eating a lot healthier. It also improved my cooking skills.

Emilio, 17 - Alejandro, 3 weeks (Donia, 15)

Your partner (and you) need food daily from the five food groups shown in **MyPyramid**:

Protein — Meat, poultry, fish, eggs, beans: 3 servings

Dairy products — milk, yogurt, cheese: 4 servings

Grains — bread, cereal, spaghetti: 6 servings

Vegetables — 3-5 servings

Fruits — 2-4 servings

If she's sick or has heartburn, eating may be a special problem. She may not be hungry at times, but she still needs to eat for the baby's sake. The baby is hungry! He must have food from the mother's blood stream continuously. If she's not sure what to eat, ask her doctor, prenatal teacher, or nutritionist.

Few of us eat a perfect diet every day. For that reason, your partner's doctor will prescribe prenatal vitamins.

Limiting the Fat

Cutting back on the fat in your food would be a good idea for both of you. **Foods high in fat include:**

- lunch meat, hot dogs
- desserts such as pie or cream puffs
- sweet rolls, doughnuts
- chips
- anything deep fried

Although each mom is different, most pregnant teens should gain between 28 and 40 pounds during pregnancy. A reducing diet at this time could harm the baby.

Pregnant teenagers often worry about gaining too much weight. If she eats a lot of junk food, she may have this problem. If she has french fries and a coke very often, she's likely to gain too much.

Instead of snacking on french fries or chips, choosing nutritious foods such as fresh fruit, peanuts, yogurt, and milk will give both of you longer lasting energy without lots of calories. These foods also give baby more energy.

The Fast Food Dilemma

If you and your partner like fast foods, you can still choose healthy items. If you decide to be a good model, for example, don't order a double bacon cheeseburger, fries, and soda. This combination is high in fat and calories and includes very little vegetables and no fruit.

Instead, try charbroiled chicken (not fried), low-fat milk, and salad. This meal provides lots of protein and a reasonable number of calories. Fat content is much lower.

Eating a lot of fast foods may mean she's getting too much sodium (salt). Pregnant women may salt food to taste, but fast foods come already salted.

Encourage her to eat the foods she needs all through pregnancy. *Your baby will thank both of you!*

Smoking Harms Fetus

When you and your partner smoke, your unborn baby does. Even being in a smoke-filled room or car is hard on a fetus. This can cause premature delivery and/or low birth weight.

> *Jennifer stopped smoking cold turkey. She was never a drinker or into drugs. We didn't go out with*

friends as much because we couldn't go places with very smoky environments.

Ryan, 17 - Katie, 7 weeks (Jennifer, 18)

Does she smoke? Perhaps you can help her stop.

If you both smoke, it helps her most if you both quit. There shouldn't be smoking around the baby.

It's hard to quit smoking, especially when you've smoked for several years. I encouraged her, and she quit cold turkey. I quit, too.

Ivan, 16 (Heather, 8 months pregnant)

Drugs and Pregnancy

If mom takes drugs during pregnancy, your child can be affected all through her life. A baby exposed to drugs before she is born may be mentally retarded. She may have other problems such as:

- learning disabilities
- language delays
- hyperactivity
- poor play skills
- other conditions that interfere with normal life

Babies who are born addicted often are handicapped. An addicted baby may be taken from his mother by Protective Services and placed in foster care.

Crack, cocaine, and crystal (crank) all have the same effects. All three cause small holes in the brain and may cause the placenta to separate early.

Effects of cocaine, crack, and crystal may not be noticed at birth. The parents may think they were lucky. Problems may not show up until the child goes to school.

Pot smoking also affects your unborn baby. This reduces the baby's oxygen supply, which can cause brain damage.

Drugs sold "over the counter" can also be a problem.

The right dose for mother means baby gets a huge overdose. Some cough and cold remedies contain alcohol. These and other common medication needs should be discussed with her doctor.

Fetal Alcohol Syndrome (FAS)

Do you and your partner like to party? If you do, she may be tempted by the alcohol and drugs. Perhaps you'll decide to help her by being a good example. If you don't drink or take drugs, it will be easier for her. You don't want her to give these things to your unborn child.

Fetal Alcohol Syndrome (FAS) affects babies whose mothers drank alcohol during pregnancy. Alcohol can hurt your baby physically and mentally. Even small amounts of beer, wine, or other alcohol can harm your baby.

An FAS baby may be too small at birth, especially in head size. Unlike most small newborns, the FAS baby never catches up.

Most have smaller than average brains. This results in some mental retardation. FAS babies are often jittery. They usually have behavior problems. Almost half of FAS babies have heart defects. These defects may mean the baby must have surgery.

Your baby's vital organs develop during early pregnancy. This is the most dangerous time of all for the mother to drink.

Bonding with Baby

If you can spend time with your partner during pregnancy, you're likely to start feeling close to baby, too . . . even before he is born. Christian agrees:

> *When Kailey was pregnant it was really weird — I'd get her from work. As soon as the baby would hear me, he'd start moving. And when I'd talk to him*

and rub Kailey's tummy, he'd just go crazy, move like crazy.

Christian, 18 - Cory, 2 (Kailey, 17)

You may already know that reading to baby has a big impact on her ability to learn. But have you considered reading to your baby *before* she is born?

We used to read to Merlalcia before she was born. I'd call Aurora and say, "Don't forget to read to her." Merlalcia loves books now.

Every night she goes, "Papa, papa," and hands me a whole bunch of books. She prefers books over the TV. I think you should read to the baby before she's born because that's what she most wants now.

Khusba

Baby Feels Crowded

Baby gains weight by making fat during the last ten weeks. She has had very little fat up to now. Fat provides energy for rapid growth. Fat also gives the body softness and curves. Fat helps baby feel cuddly to us. It also protects baby from heat and cold.

Baby can live outside at this time. However, he is not ready to be born. If he's born before 36 weeks gestation, he will have to stay in the hospital "finishing" his development. This may take ten to twelve weeks. Babies born too early often have problems. Some tiny babies outgrow these problems. Others do not.

At 40 weeks, the average baby weights 7 1/2 pounds and is 20-22 inches long. His mother has gained at least 25 pounds during pregnancy. Your baby is now ready for life on the outside.

You Have an Important Task

Pregnant teenagers tend to grow up fast. They must deal with the physical changes of pregnancy, and they are facing other great changes in their lives.

If you aren't close during the pregnancy, it may be hard for you to understand. Even if you're with her, you may still find it hard to deal with her moodiness. She may not be as much fun as she was. As the months go by, she may focus more and more on her baby.

> *The father has an important job during pregnancy — to support her. We'd fight a lot, but I'd never tell her she looked bad. When they're pregnant, they have real low self-esteem anyway, and you have to be supportive, completely supportive.*
>
> *If you aren't getting along, agree to disagree. Even if you've split up and don't like each other, you have a kid together. You have to support each other.*
>
> Zach

Parents who support each other are doing their child a favor.

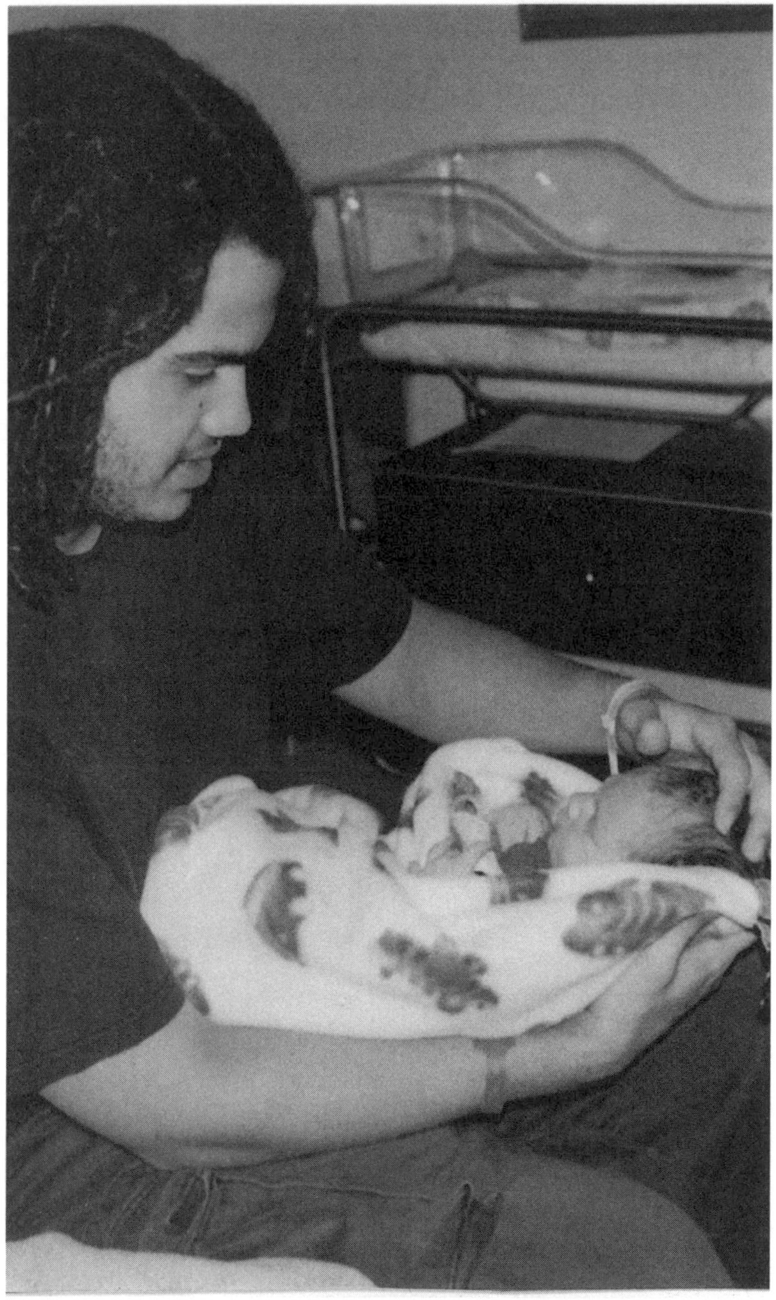

"When I finally saw her, she was so beautiful."

4

The Birth of Your Baby

- **Preparing for childbirth**
- **She may have "false labor"**
- **Early signs of labor**
- **Role of her coach**
- **Timing her contractions**
- **Your baby is born**
- **Your newborn's appearance**
- **Delivery of the placenta**
- **For some, a C-section**
- **Baby's first test**

One day she's having these cramps. I didn't think it was anything so I went to work. She called me at work, "Christian, I'm having the baby." My brother-in-law picked me up and Kailey was in the car. I didn't know what to do. We get there, they take her in. He was born three hours later.

I cut the umbilical cord — a very new experience for me. We couldn't hold him at first because he was cold and they put him in an incubator for 30 minutes. Then we got to hold him and she breastfed him.

Christian, 18 - Cory, 2, (Kailey, 17)

The night Jocelyn went into labor we were celebrating our anniversary. We were sitting there, and she said she was having a lot of pains. I called the doctor, and we were at the hospital in 10 minutes.

She was in labor for 11 hours.

When I cut the cord, a tear dropped out of my eyes. I looked at the baby and I was amazed. I was happy, really happy.

Tim, 20 - Chamique, 21 months (Jocelyn, 19)

Lynette's water broke about 6 a.m. I was nervous although I stayed awful calm. We went to the hospital right away, and they put us in this room for four or five hours. It wasn't like scary, but I see Lynette in pain, and I couldn't do anything about it. In my mind I was hoping nothing wrong would happen.

They put us in the delivery room and I saw the whole thing. I saw Sophie come out, and the first thing she did was open her eyes. She didn't cry until later. It was the most beautiful thing in the world to see how life is happening.

Later on I went in to see Lynette, and they brought Sophie in. She was so little and tiny and I was scared to touch.

Jacob, 19 - Sophie, 7 months (Lynette, 18)

Your partner is probably thinking about labor and delivery by the time she's five or six months pregnant. Some mothers describe their baby's birth as a high point in life while others are much more negative. Each person's experience is different.

Preparing for Childbirth

Taking a prepared childbirth class with your partner is a good plan. Sign up early because the class may fill up quickly. If you can be her coach during labor and delivery, you can help her handle your baby's birth more positively. Most hospitals these days are family-centered, encouraging coaches to be with the mother during labor, delivery, and recovery. Check with her healthcare provider or hospital for the number of people that can be with her during the birth.

If her mom or her girlfrend (or both) want to coach her, let them share.

Labor contractions used to be called pains. When she's having a contraction, it feels like her uterus is making a fist. Her belly gets hard as the baby pushes it. The contractions help push the baby out.

Contractions can cause discomfort and, for some women, quite a bit of pain. If you take prepared childbirth classes together, you will both learn the best way for her to breathe through her contractions to make labor and delivery easier for her.

She will also learn relaxation exercises that will help her prepare for labor and delivery. You can practice these exercises with her.

> *The prepared childbirth class helped me a lot. It showed me what to expect. I learned how to breathe, and how to pace myself. Each time a contraction came, I tried to be calm.*
>
> *If you think it's going to be horrible, it will be worse. If you keep calm, it's not as painful or as hard.*
>
> Delia, 16 - Kelsey, 7 months (Randy, 17)

Prepared childbirth doesn't mean any one "method" such as Lamaze. There are several different methods. Sometimes prepared childbirth is called "natural" childbirth. This does not mean she can't have medicine to ease the pain. With preparation, however, she may not need a lot of help from drugs.

You and your partner should talk to her doctor about pain relief during labor. She needs to know her choices before labor begins. Even if she doesn't want drugs during labor/delivery, you both should learn about her choices.

If she needs pain relief medication, she may be given an *epidural*. This is a process in which the anesthesiologist places a soft rubber catheter in her lower back. A medication similar to what a dentist uses to lessen dental pain is then injected. This causes numbness from below her umbilicus (belly button) down into her legs.

She May Have "False Labor"

During the last few weeks of pregnancy, your partner's body is getting ready for the baby's birth. Her uterus may begin practicing for this big event. She may feel early contractions. These early "false labor" contractions are called Braxton-Hicks or pre-term contractions. If she can relax and work with the baby now, she's likely to have less discomfort when real labor begins.

Some moms don't have these pre-labor contractions. Others have them off and on for several weeks. If this is real labor, her contractions won't go away.

Early Signs of Labor

During pregnancy, a woman's cervix (opening to the uterus) is sealed with a mucous plug. This plug keeps germs in her vagina from getting in her uterus. If germs could reach the unborn baby, they could give him an infection.

When this plug comes out, it's a sign that labor day is soon. Some mothers, however, never notice the mucous plug. Their labor may begin when the bag of water breaks. This is the sac that lines the uterus where the baby grows.

When this happens, she'll feel a gush of warm water. It keeps coming out no matter how hard she tries to stop it.

Tara was in a flea market with her mom when her water broke at about 11 a.m. They called me at school, and I left. She stayed home until 1:30. Her aunt, her mom, and I drove her to the hospital.

About 8:00 that night they gave her a drug to start contractions. By 10:30 they were getting real sharp, and Alexis was born at 12:38. I was there when she was born. It's hard to describe — it's wonderful because it's part of you. Watching Tara go through the pain was the hard part.

The doctor asked if I wanted to cut the umbilical cord, and I said, "Sure." It's amazing.

When they let Tara hold Alexis, it was great. I was videotaping the whole thing.

Dennis, 17 - Alexis, 6 months (Tara, 20)

For still other women, contractions are the signal that labor is beginning. Or she may have a backache and feel "heavy" when labor starts. Using prepared childbirth exercises at this time usually helps.

Role of Her Coach

Most important is that you be there to encourage her during labor. The coach can help in several ways:

- Assure her she is not alone.
- Comfort her. Make her feel as good as you can.
- Give her both emotional and physical support.
- Help communicate to her and from her to others.
- Remind her of the "tools" she learned in childbirth preparation class and of the "tricks" you remember from that class.

Be there with her all the way. Lend her your eyes filled with love, your smiles filled with encouragement. Provide her with as much comfort as you possibly can:

- Lend her your hands to help take away the pain. Massage her back, feet, or wherever she wishes. Get her whatever she needs.

- Lend her as much emotional support for as long as she needs it. Communicate your feelings to her in a loving, caring, warm way. Give her your strength.

Give her the technical assistance that you both learned in your preparation class:

- Relaxation — breathing patterns
- Concentration — knowledge versus fear
- Positions for labor and delivery

You need to do only what you can do or will feel comfortable doing. No one expects you to know everything or remember what will work or not work. If you're not sure, ask the nurse. But remember, this is the birth of your baby.

They called me at 3:30 a.m. Me and my mom went up to the hospital. I went into the room and Marie was lying in bed. At first I felt nauseous because I don't like needles and they gave her Demerol.

Marie was in labor for eight hours. I held her hand the whole time, giving her ice chips, putting cold cloths on her head.

Actually, I was excited. It was the best feeling watching my baby being born. I cut the umbilical cord, and it was the best experience. After everything was done, I rocked the baby.

Josh, 18 - Amber, 21/2 months (Marie, 16)

Timing Her Contractions

When her contractions start, you or someone else should time them. How far apart are they? Check the time from the beginning of one contraction until the next one begins. This is the interval.

How long do they last? Check the time from the beginning of the contraction until it stops. This is called the duration. Your doctor will ask about both the interval and duration.

When she arrives at the hospital, she'll go to a labor room, and you can probably go with her. The nurse will likely place a fetal monitor low on her stomach. This is a machine for measuring contractions. It shows how long, how hard, and how often contractions come. It also keeps track of the baby's pulse.

The doctor or nurse will frequently measure the progress of your baby by checking Mom's cervix for dilation.

The last period of labor is called transition. Her contractions are hard and coming often. At this point, her labor is almost over. She's moving toward delivery of your baby.

The baby moves down into the birth canal. He prepares to come out. In most hospitals the labor room is also the birthing room and the place where Mom will recover from your baby's birth.

During delivery she'll be in a position like the one for a pelvic check-up. The head of the bed will be up like a chair and the foot of the bed drops away to allow for the delivery.

She may have chills. If she does, ask for a blanket to cover her legs and body. It isn't really cold. It's a hormonal change that prepares her for delivery.

After she's in position, the doctor may wash the birthing area. He will carefully watch the baby's progress. They will check the baby's heart rate often. Don't be alarmed if they give mom some oxygen to help the baby. They are simply making sure things go well for both mom and baby.

It was a long night – she was in labor 121/2 hours. It was scary at times, seeing how much pain she was in. You get to feeling guilty.

I sat there and told her to breathe. She had an epidural, but she was awake for most of it. It was rough. I didn't think it would be that bad.

When she was born, I felt proud.

Matt, 19 - Destini, 6 months (Violet, 17)

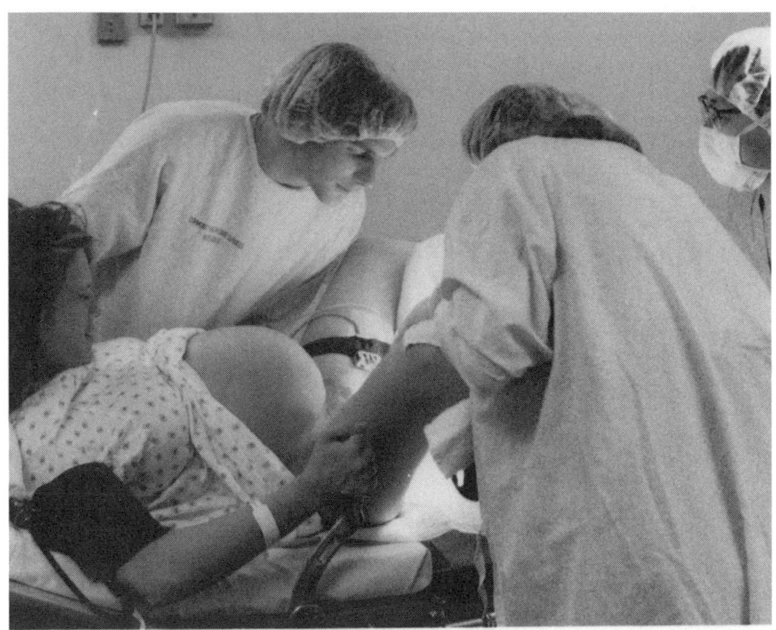

Your baby is coming!

When the doctor or midwife decides it's time, she'll tell Mom to push when she's having a contraction. This feels like the urge to have a bowel movement.

Pushing too soon may make the cervix swell. This can slow things down. It also puts pressure on baby's head.

I walked with Claudia to the delivery room and put on the scrub suit. I was there, and when they were telling her to push, it felt like I was doing it, too. I was doing everything the doctor told her to do.

Then I saw the head, and they pulled her out. It was like I was all a part of it, too.

Adam, 17 - Brittaney, 10 months (Claudia, 18)

When the head of the baby appears, it's described as crowning. What a lovely word! Someone important is being crowned — your baby.

It usually takes less than an hour of pushing to bring

your baby out. Three good pushes with each contraction are suggested. Many mothers say this is the most exciting part.

Right before delivery, the doctor may do an episiotomy. This is a small cut made to make the vaginal opening bigger for delivery of your baby. Sometimes doctors do it to avoid the chance of having the tissue tear. Or he may massage her perineum (area between her vagina and rectum) to help the opening stretch over the baby's head.

Your Baby Is Born

In the delivery room it was kind of scary. There was a lot of blood. Alexis was going through pain. I could see it in her face, and she grabbed my hand.

Then all of a sudden my baby's head started pushing out. At first she didn't want to come out, she kept going back in. Then suddenly my daughter was born.

The doctor asked me if I wanted to cut her umbilical cord. At first I said no because I thought it would hurt her, but they said it wouldn't. So I cut it. It was kind of hard to cut.

It's a lot of experience to be there, kind of scary, and I was happy.

Isaac, 18 - Brooke, 9 months (Alexis, 17)

With crowning, the baby goes from mom's body into our world. At first, you'll see just a little of baby's head, then more and more until the whole head slips out and turns to the side. Baby's shoulders come out one at a time. Then the rest of the body comes quickly. This all takes less than five minutes!

During the later stages of pregnancy I got real scared because I started thinking of all the complications. That was the biggest scare of my life, because I wanted the baby to be all right. Then when Kevin started to come out, I was even more scared. Please don't let anything be wrong. I was so scared.

The head came out, and then the whole body. I immediately counted all the fingers and toes, then looked at which sex it was.

By this time I was ecstatic. My eyes were watering. It was such an experience.

The nurse laid Kevin on Erica's chest. I cut the cord, I kissed Erica, and said, "Congratulations. You did a good job." Then I held Kevin. I knew then it was all worth it.

Zach, 19 - Kevin, 20 months (Erica, 16)

You and mom will feel lots of excitement. You'll find out whether you had a boy or a girl (if you don't already know from the ultrasound picture). You'll learn about the condition of your new person. The doctor may let you assist him by cutting the cord.

It didn't really hit Jumana until after the baby was born, and she was crying in the hospital. It hit me the same way although I didn't cry. It was all these emotions hitting at the same time.

Shane, 16 - Burke, 61/2 months (Jumana, 15)

Your Newborn's Appearance

Your just-born baby may look red, wrinkled, and worried. You and his mother, however, are likely to think he's the most beautiful baby ever born.

Seeing Katie come out, I cried. It was just amazing. I never had any physical contact with her like Jennifer did during pregnancy. When I finally saw Katie, I broke down in tears, she was so beautiful.

Ryan, 17 - Katie, 7 weeks (Jennifer, 18)

His head may be "molded" during delivery. Instead of looking round, it may seem too long. He may have strange lumps on his head, too. At birth, the bones in baby's head are soft. This allows his head to change shape slightly as it goes through the birth canal. Soon his head will become round again.

The baby will sometimes come out with white cream-like lotion covering his body. This is called vernix, and it protects baby's skin during his nine months in the water.

Often babies come out blue-purple in color, then turn to grey-white, then to pinkish brown.

At birth, black babies' skin is often lighter than it will be later. The skin at the tip of the ear is close to the baby's "real" color. Their fingers and toes sometimes take longer to get their final color.

When your baby cries, his skin may turn red and blotchy. This, too, is normal.

Some babies cry immediately. Others need to have mucous or amniotic fluid removed first. The nurse will gently remove these fluids from baby's mouth and nose with a bulb syringe.

Sometimes baby comes out with some of the mother's blood on him.

Delivery of the Placenta

The delivery of the placenta or afterbirth completes the birth process. The placenta has fed your baby for nearly nine months. It now separates from the uterine wall and comes out. This happens within 15 minutes of delivery.

If necessary, the doctor repairs mom's episiotomy with a few stitches. Large sanitary napkins are put on her. She'll have a very heavy period-like flow of blood for a few days, but this is not her regular period.

It takes about six weeks for the spot where the placenta was to heal. *Nothing* should enter her vagina until she has completely healed.

For Some, a C-section

Caesarean section (C-section): *Birth of child by cutting through walls of abdomen.*

Kim had preterm labor and the toxemia got pretty bad to where it endangered the baby. She stayed in the hospital for five days before Kianna was born. During this time I was scared. I couldn't help her.

Her blood pressure was up, and it was a hard time. She had a C-section because Kianna was breech.

Daric, 16 - Kianna, 1 year (Kim, 18)

About one in five moms has a Caesarean section. Reasons for doing a C-section include:

- The baby is too big compared to the mother's size (called "fetal pelvic disproportion").
- Labor slows down or stops.
- Certain types of infections occur such as herpes.
- Placenta previa (placenta covers inner cervix).
- Fetal distress (baby is in danger) or maternal distress (mom is in danger).
- The position of the baby is a problem. It may be breech (bottom first) or transverse (sideways).
- Failure to dilate enough for baby's head to go through birth canal (called "failure to progress").
- Prematurity.

Labor and delivery was pretty crazy. It was weird. Tiffany had high blood pressure and they said they'd have to keep us overnight. They decided to induce labor. I was going to go home and sleep, but they called me right back to tell me she had to have it C-section.

It wasn't fun, but it was very quick. I watched through it all. It was pretty hard. I think it was difficult for us both.

Zaid, 19 - Amber, 15 months (Tiffany, 20)

When he actually came out and I saw him crying, it was one of the happiest moments of my life. It's a moment you feel real good about.

Shane

Your Baby's First Test

The nurse will measure your baby's responses. This test is called the Apgar score. It's given to baby right after he's born. He'll be tested again after a few minutes. Scores range from 0 to 10. Most babies score between 6 and 9.

The Apgar test measures:

- color
- pulse
- cry
- movements
- strength of breathing

The nurse will weigh and measure your baby and wrap her in a blanket. She may give her back to you for awhile. She may then take her to the nursery for observation. You can probably go with your baby to the nursery.

I remember just looking at her. This is so weird, this is part of me, this is ours. It was scary though, because I realized I had something depending on me. It was scary. All my life I depended on someone else. I still was, and now somebody depended on me.

Zach

Your life has changed!

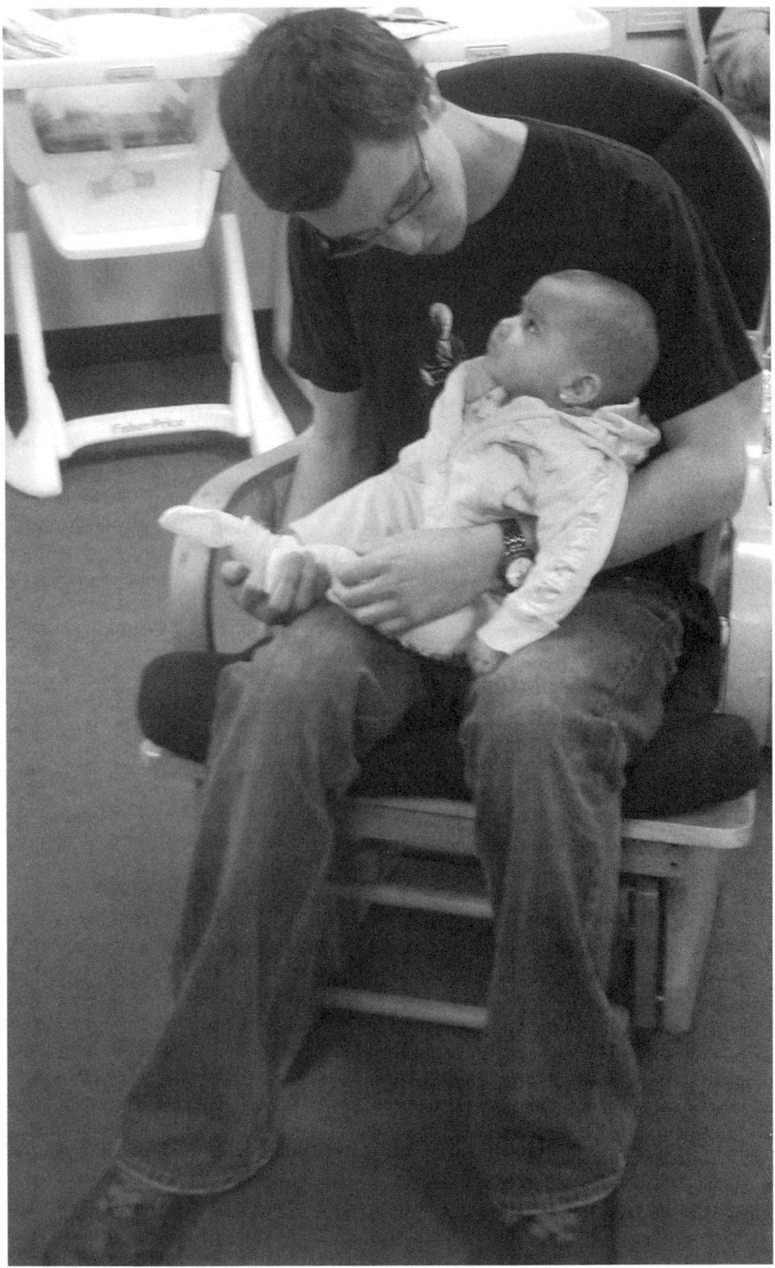

"I was over there every day in shock and amazement that this is my baby." (Shane)

5

Caring for Your Newborn

- Those first days
- Getting to know baby
- Partner relationship
- Breastfeeding is best
- How often will she eat?
- No propped bottles
- Infants don't "spoil"
- Important note
- Babies and colic
- Dealing with diaper rash
- Some babies have special needs
- Can you take a parenting class?
- Staying involved
- A wonderful challenge

When Jumana came home with Burke, I was over there every day, in shock and amazement that this is my baby.

Shane, 16 - Burke, 61/2 months (Jumana, 15)

He's three weeks old now — I go see him every day after school. He doesn't cry that much. When he cries, I hold him. I learned in the labor and delivery class how to hold him in a position that gets him comfortable, how to fold the blanket, etc., to help him sleep.

Emilio, 17 - Alejandro, 3 weeks (Donia, 15)

Those first two months are frustrating because they cry.

I'd try to feed him, and he wouldn't eat, and I'd get more frustrated. You have to realize it's going to be like that. You have to be real strong in the mind and keep your cool. It's hard.

I wasn't able to sleep because every 15 minutes I'd have to stand up and check on Braxton that first week. They don't sleep quietly — they don't even sleep.

In the middle of the night Susanne wouldn't wake up. She would cover herself with a pillow — it was too much for her. It would make me mad because she wasn't strong. I felt like she wasn't doing enough, like she had the baby and she didn't care any more.

I'd sit down with Braxton, and I'd hold him. I'd sing to him and play my guitar. For awhile it was a problem because I wasn't getting enough rest. I missed a lot of school.

Antonio, 16 - Braxton, 4 months (Susanne, 15)

Those First Days

We shared the night feedings. Luckily Dustin started sleeping through the night real soon. We did it all together. I don't think it would be fair if I just said I'm not getting up, I'm not going to give him a bottle. We shared the responsibility of having him. I think you have to go 50-50.

Mark, 22 - Dustin, 21/2 (Kelly Ellen, 20)

Both you and your partner will probably be very tired the first few weeks after your baby is born. You'll lose sleep when the baby is awake at night. Your partner will be even more tired because of the hormonal changes going on as her body returns to its non-pregnant state.

If she had an episiotomy, her stitches will hurt for a few days after delivery. She'll have a discharge called lochia for two to six weeks after the baby is born.

Partly because of her hormonal changes, she may feel sad part of the time during those first weeks. This happens so often that doctors label the condition after-baby blues.

The best cure for after-baby blues is help with child care. Encourage your partner to do something for herself. Better yet, can someone else watch the baby for an hour or two while the two of you go out together? Or the three of you could get out and do something together as a new family, perhaps go to the mall or visit friends.

If her depression lasts more than a week or two, encourage her to check with her healthcare provider.

Getting to Know Your Baby

Going home from the hospital was weird. It wasn't reality to me that I was a father. It took me about a week, and then it hit me — my son kept crying, waking me up in the middle of the night, and we had to get up and rock him. I was scared, but the first month was exciting.

I've been without my father all my life and I want to make sure Avery has a father. I think if I'd had a father I'd have acted different. I'd have had the discipline I needed, and I wouldn't have gotten into the trouble I've had. You know, to teach the male things.

Todd, 18 - Avery, 6 months (Celia, 19)

The most important part of caring for your baby is getting to know her — bonding together as closely as possible. Bonding with your baby can be described as falling in love.

When you put your finger across your newborn baby's palm, she'll grab it firmly. She seems to be saying, "I need you so much." You'll feel a tug at your heart strings.

If you interact a lot with baby — hold her, talk to her, carry on conversations whenever she's awake — you'll find the bonding happens just the way it should.

When Burke was a tiny baby, I'd sit there and talk to him and caress the top of his head. Now we rock. We'll sit there and he plays with toys until he gets tired.

Shane

If you haven't had much experience with tiny infants, let your partner show you how to diaper, feed, and rock baby. With practice, you'll feel confident.

Safety Note

When you put your baby down to sleep by herself, always place her on her back. This helps prevent SIDS (Sudden Infant Death Syndrome).

You are your baby's first and most important "toy." She will stare into your eyes for a long time. Remember — self-concept is developed by how people respond to us. Both you and her mom lay the foundation for that development.

Your Relationship with Your Partner

Have you wondered what sex will be like after childbirth? You may wonder how long you have to wait. Your partner may worry about whether it will hurt. She may not want to do it very soon. She may be so tired those first weeks after delivery that she has no interest in sex.

Couples generally are advised to wait for the six-week checkup before having intercourse after childbirth. Her vaginal tissue may still be tender the first few times. Each of you needs to be patient with the other. If she's breastfeeding, her breasts may be sensitive, and she may not want them to be touched as much. The vaginal opening will be about the same size it was before she got pregnant. At first, juices that help keep the area moist may not be working well. A water-based lubricant such as KY jelly will help.

It's very important to remember that four weeks to six months after delivery, the mother's first egg will be released without warning. This happens before her first regular period has arrived. Therefore, she can get pregnant the first time you have sex. Make sure you're protected!

Breastfeeding Is Best

Many young mothers and dads choose breast milk for their babies. They know this is the best possible food for their baby:

- No waiting
- Protects baby against germs — he's less likely to get sick.
- Easier to digest
- Tastes better to baby

It's also easier for mom and dad — no bottles to sterilize, no formula to mix, and no bottles to heat. This can make life simpler for a tired new mother. Breastfeeding is also cheaper than buying formula.

Whether or not mom and the baby are receiving financial help from Social Services, they might be eligible for help from WIC (Special Supplemental Feeding Program for Women, Infants, and Children). Call your Public Health Department for information. They may be able to get coupons for certain foods mom needs if she's pregnant or breastfeeding, and for formula for baby if he's bottle-fed.

The Food Stamp Program helps extend food dollars for eligible families. Ask your social worker for information.

The American Academy of Pediatrics (AAP) recommends breastfeeding for the first six months for all babies, and for the first year if possible. Babies who are breastfed tend to be healthier than babies given formula.

Of course your baby's mother will decide whether she'll breastfeed or not, but you can encourage her to make this

Breast milk provides the best food possible for your baby.

choice for your baby.

A breastfeeding mother needs to take good care of herself. She should continue eating the same good foods she needed during pregnancy plus drink extra liquids.

Breastfeeding is likely to work better for mother and baby if baby is given no bottles during the first month. By the second month, however, give baby a bottle once in a while. There may be a time when mom won't be with her, and she'll need to know how to take a bottle. Giving her a bottle gives you a chance to feed her.

> *Aurora breastfed for a year. Sometimes she'd pump out the milk and put it in the refrigerator so I could give Merlalcia a bottle.*
>
> Khusba, 22 - Merlalcia, 11/2 yr. (Aurora, 17)

You can do the burping. You can put her to sleep in your arms after she's eaten.

If you use formula, simply follow the directions on the package or can of formula. For awhile, baby will probably prefer his formula heated to body temperature.

Heating baby's bottle in the microwave oven is a dangerous practice. While the bottle may feel cool, the formula inside could be hot enough to burn your baby. It's better to heat the bottle of formula in a pan of hot water or use an electric bottle warmer.

You can bathe her — or perhaps you and mom will make those first baths a team project. You'll also share in the comforting when baby is unhappy. In fact, whether or not mom breastfeeds, you'll find lots of ways to bond with your infant.

The first time I had to change him was an experience I won't forget. I had never changed a baby before. It was weird because I never had to watch over anyone, something so small that was mine. Before, I hadn't even worried about myself, and now I have to give him a lot of my attention.

Andy, 17 - Gus, 5 months (Yolanda, 15)

Changing your baby can also be fun. This is about the only time a newborn is awake, aware, and not eating. Your baby is learning a lot about her world. Make sure that during those early days she sees your face and hears your voice as often as possible.

Warning

Never leave baby alone on a changing table, bed, or other off-the-floor surface for a second. The baby who couldn't turn over yesterday may do so today.

We usually change him on the floor because he's rolling now. We don't put him on tables at all.

Bill, 19 - Billy, 6 months (Jan, 17)

How Often Will She Eat?

How often should baby be fed? Whenever she's hungry! Babies can't tell time yet. They need to be fed when they're hungry, and their hunger pains have nothing to do with the clock. And they *don't* cry to exercise their lungs!

At times, baby won't finish her bottle. You don't need to worry — she probably wasn't as hungry as usual. Her appetite will vary from feeding to feeding. "Enough" at one meal may not be enough next time.

Unless baby is totally breastfed, offer him a bottle of water occasionally, especially in hot weather. Use bottled water or water you've boiled and cooled. Don't add sugar.

No Propped Bottles — Ever

Whenever you give your baby a bottle, always be sure you hold him. Don't ever lay him down and prop his bottle in his mouth, then leave him to drink alone.

First of all, he needs the love and emotional support he'll feel from being in your arms or his mother's.

Second, many ear infections are caused by baby drinking from a propped bottle. The passageway from the ear to the throat doesn't drain well in infancy. Milk, if not "served" properly, can go back to his ears and cause an infection.

Third, a propped bottle is dangerous for infants. Baby could choke from his milk coming too fast from that propped bottle. He could also choke on milk curds if he should spit up. He might be unable to clear his throat.

Some babies need burping several times during a feeding while others don't want or need their meal interrupted. Several burping positions work:

— Hold him upright against your shoulder.

— Support him in a sitting position on your lap.

— Lay him on his stomach across your knees.

Whichever position you choose, rub or pat his back gently until he burps. For many babies, this happens fairly quickly, while others need several minutes of help with the important job of burping.

Babies need a lot of sucking, sometimes more than they

get from the bottle or breast. It's okay for baby to suck on his fist or thumb. And it's okay to offer him a pacifier. Just don't substitute the pacifier for the attention, food, or diaper changes he wants and needs when he's crying.

Infants Don't "Spoil"

Avery cried a lot. I'd pick him up and rock him, talk to him as much as I could. That's the only way you can quiet a baby is to rock him to sleep, sing to him, talk to him. That's mainly what I did, talk to him, bounce him gently.

Some people told me every time he cried I shouldn't pick him up. I just said I don't want to let him cry. If he's crying, something is wrong. He cries for a reason.

Todd

You ask, "Should I pick her up when she cries? Won't she think she can get whatever she wants by crying?"

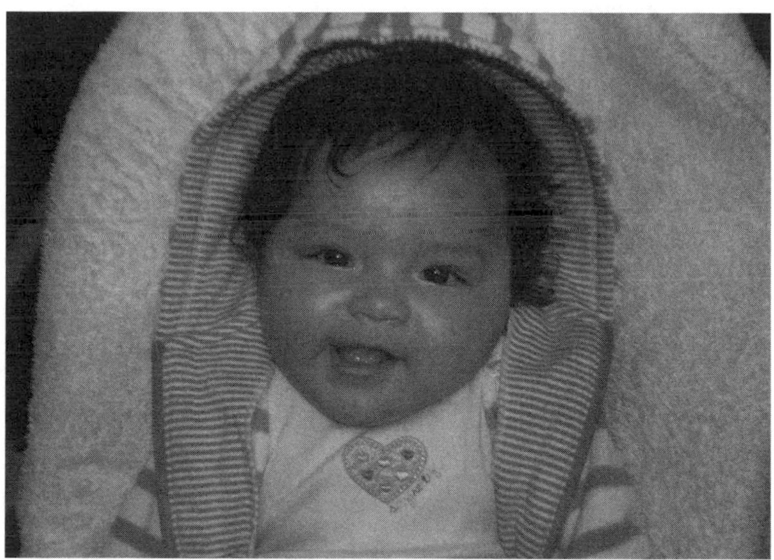

*When you meet her needs, you're teaching her to trust you. You're **not** spoiling her!*

This old idea simply isn't true. Yes, she'll cry when she needs something. She will also learn from the parent who answers her cries. She'll learn a basic sense of trust in her world. That sense of trust is the most important thing she can learn during her first months.

> *When Breanna cried, I'd pick her up, walk around with her, give her a bottle. When I'd stand up with her, Breanna stopped crying. She still likes me holding her. That felt real good when she'd quit crying when I picked her up. She knew she was safe.*
>
> Hugo, 16 — Breanna, 9 months (Marcella, 18)

Most parents love holding their baby. Touch her, love her. Don't worry about spoiling her in these early months. Babies under six months of age don't cry because they're spoiled. They cry because they need something, and crying is the only way they can "talk" to you. Have you noticed how her cries sound different depending on what she seems to need or want?

Even if you've fed and changed her, and you know she's neither too warm nor too cold, she may still cry. Often it's because she's lonely. Or she may be a colicky baby who just cries more than some babies do.

Nearly every baby loves to be touched, held, and cuddled. Your baby snuggling into your arms makes both of you feel good.

When baby is fussy, hold her upright. Put her head near your shoulder. When she's there, she can hear your heart beat. This may quiet her. It may even put her to sleep.

Important Note

Sometimes you'll do everything you can to help your baby be comfortable, and she'll still cry. Always remember she is *not* crying to upset you. She isn't crying because you've spoiled her. She's crying because it's the only way she can tell you that she wants you.

Perhaps taking her outside will help. She may stop crying if she has something new and different to watch. A ride in the car (safely secured in her car seat) may calm her. Some parents report their babies fall asleep almost the instant the car starts.

Some babies go to sleep most easily when they're in their swing. Soft music might help. A little music box beside their bed soothes some babies.

Sometimes your baby will cry because she doesn't feel well. Is she feverish? Is she teething? See Chapter 8 for more about caring for baby when she's not feeling well.

If your bottle-fed baby cries a lot, perhaps her formula isn't right for her. Talk with your healthcare provider. Perhaps s/he will suggest a different formula.

As you get to know your baby, you'll find still other ways to help her be more comfortable.

> *I go to a parenting class, and the teacher said when you place a baby on your bare chest, she'll stop crying. I tried that, and it worked.*
>
> Jamal, 16 - Valizette, 16 months (Shawnté, 17)

Try Jamal's suggestion when your baby is crying. Feeling your skin against hers may soothe her and make her feel better.

Babies and Colic

Some babies cry and cry, and it seems impossible to comfort them. Such a baby may have colic. If he does, he may seem to have a stomach ache and have attacks of crying nearly every evening.

His face may suddenly become red; he'll frown, draw up his legs, and scream loudly. When you pick him up and try to comfort him, he keeps screaming, perhaps for 15 to 20 minutes. Just as he is about to fall asleep, he may start screaming again. He may pass some gas.

No one knows what causes colic. It generally comes at about the same time every day. During the rest of the day, the colicky baby will probably be happy, alert, eat well, and gain weight.

If your baby seems to have colic, check with your doctor to see if anything else is wrong. If not, make sure baby isn't hungry, wet, cold, or lonely. During an attack of colic, holding him on his stomach across your knees may comfort him. Sometimes giving him a warm bath helps.

The good news about colic is that baby will grow out of it by the time he is about three months old. In the meantime, he will be harder to live with because of his colic. Comfort him as best you can, and look forward to the time his colic ends.

Dealing with Diaper Rash

Occasionally babies get diaper rash when taking antibiotics. A second cause may be an allergy to the ingredients in a particular brand of diaper.

Baby can be comforted by warm cloths to the area. You can also sprinkle cornstarch carefully on the reddened area.

Rashes caused by an antibiotic may require a prescription ointment. Be sure to ask the healthcare provider for a prescription ointment next time an antibiotic is recommended for your baby.

It's easier to prevent diaper rash than it is to get rid of it. For your baby's comfort — and your own — change her often. And you need to clean her thoroughly each time you change her.

Some Babies Have Special Needs

For a few parents, their newborn baby may bring special challenges. It may be a short-term problem.

Most parents who are told their baby has a special need find it hard to believe at first. Once the fact sinks in that something really could be wrong, many parents become eager to find a cure for the problem.

Others try to find out why, and even occasionally want to blame someone for what has happened. All these feelings are natural, but problems can arise between a couple when one partner blames the other for the baby's condition. Other parents become depressed.

You'll probably find talking these feelings over with a person who has facts about the baby's condition helps. This could be your doctor, a nurse, the social worker at the hospital, your priest, minister, rabbi, or imam.

It also could be a person from one of the many public and private community agencies that help families with special babies. If your baby should have special needs, don't be afraid to ask for help in understanding what has happened.

Zaid talked about his daughter, who was born two months early:

> *Amber weighed three pounds, fourteen ounces, and was born with a cleft lip and cleft palate. We had the surgery for the cleft lip when she was about five months old, and for the cleft palate several months later.*
>
> *People should realize how lucky they are to have their baby with no problem. I think they take it for granted.*
>
> *We went to the cleft palate meetings where they bring specialists, and we learned how to treat our baby. For instance, we had to have special nipples for her bottles. We made sure we knew as much as possible about what was happening.*
>
> Zaid, 19 - Amber, 15 months (Tiffany, 20)

For more information on special needs babies, see *Your Pregnancy and Newborn Journey*, chapter 9.

Can You Take a Parenting Class?

Is there a parenting class at your school? Or does your adult school offer evening classes on infant care? Attending a good parenting class will help you feel more confident as you care for your child.

> *Fathers need to get into classes like this so they can really know about the baby. Some men, when they find out she's pregnant, leave because they don't know nothing about it. If they learn what it's like, they're more likely to stay. This baby will be part of your life until you die. You need to know what you're doing.*
>
> Agie, 18 - Mia, 1 month (Shalaine, 18)

If possible, attend parenting class together with your baby's mother. Many schools offer classes especially for school-age parents.

Some of the young men quoted in this book attend such a class. They talk about how to care for their babies. They also find support from the other young parents in the class.

Staying Involved with Your Child

More and more fathers are realizing how much better their relationship with their child is if they're deeply involved in caring for that child from the start. They know that if only mom takes care of the baby, dad misses out.

> *The first time I drove with Katie in the car I was very nervous. Coming home with her was a little different because Jennifer and I weren't going to our own home. It was okay. Now she's within biking distance and I come up here as often as I want.*
>
> Ryan, 17 - Katie, 7 weeks (Jennifer, 18)

If you don't live with your baby and his mother, you still need to be as involved as possible in his care. Make the most of the time you have with your child. Change him, feed him, rock him, play with him, and enjoy him.

If mom doesn't seem to want you to see much of your child, talk with her. Sometimes it's hard to communicate feelings about something as important as parenting your child. You're more likely to be heard if you:

- Talk when you aren't upset.
- Keep to the subject — the welfare of your child.
- Don't get sidetracked into fighting with each other.

Your baby's mom may not understand how you feel. It's important that you speak up — in a friendly way — and tell her how important parenting your child is to you.

Whether you're with your baby's mother or not, you and baby will be ahead if you're involved in baby care. When you are, everyone wins. Mom will have some of the help she needs with baby. The more you do with baby, the faster you'll bond with your child. Your baby wins by having two loving parents.

You Have a Wonderful Challenge

The first months with a new baby offer a real challenge to his parents. Your major task is simply to meet his needs as much as possible.

> *Babies need a lot of attention. They need all the love you can give, and all the attention. If they don't feel the love from you, they won't feel secure and safe.*
>
> Khusba

So feed him when he's hungry. Change him when he's wet. Talk to him, hold him when he's lonely. *He'll reward you by responding to you more and more as the days go by.*

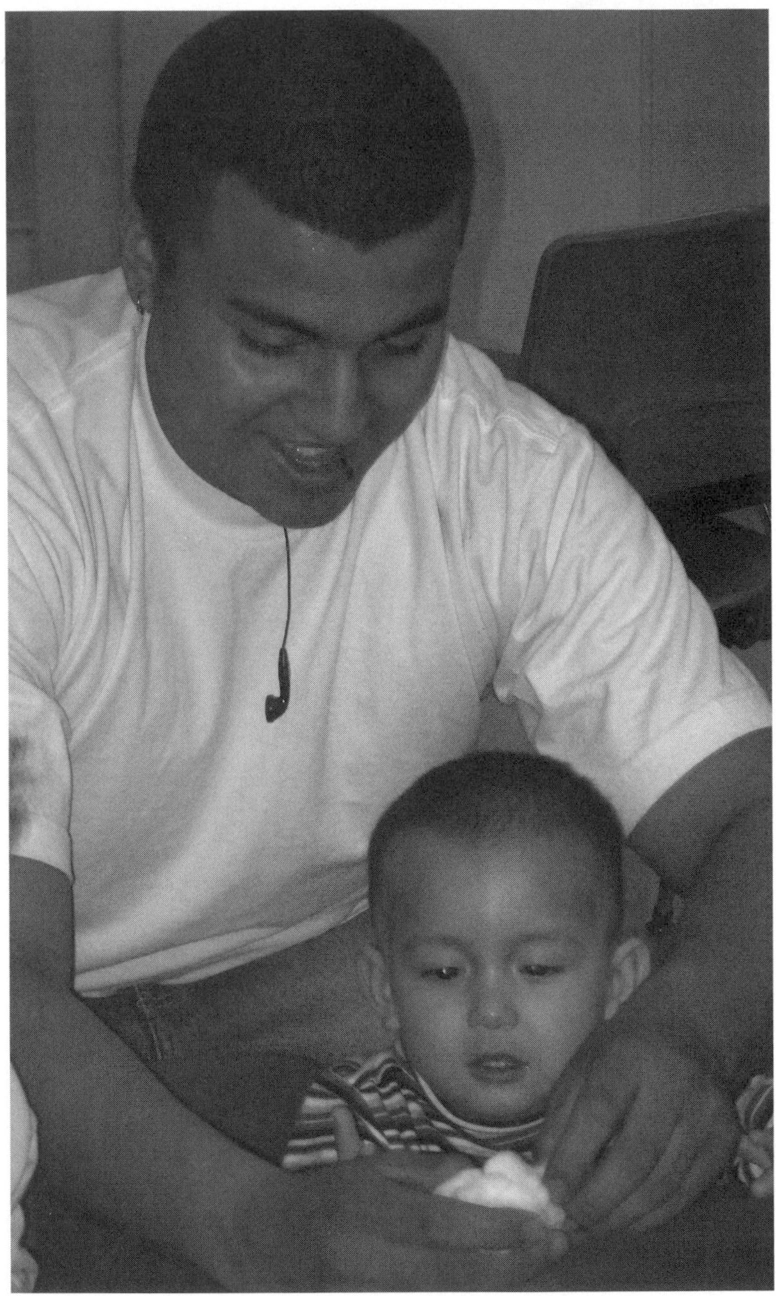

He needs lots of attention now.

6

When He's Crawling — Watch Out!

- **Toys for baby**
- **Build trust by responding**
- **Baby's fears**
- **Stranger anxiety**
- **She listens and "talks"**
- **Curiosity leads to crawling**
- **Your baby starts teething**
- **Nursing bottle syndrome**
- **Bedtime routine is important**
- **Playing together**

Now Burke is getting to the stage where he hits stuff . . . He's a chubby guy with beautiful eyes. Everyone says he's the spitting image of me. I have him about every weekend, and during the week I go over and check up on him. He has a smile that lights me up when I see it. It gives me a very good feeling. I love him to death.

Shane, 16 - Burke, 61/2 months
(Jumana, 15)

Sophie sits up very well now. She doesn't crawl, but she's trying to walk. She goes wherever she wants by hopping. She wants to stand up all the time.

We put her on the floor and give her toys. After fifteen minutes she gets bored. She likes plastic cups better than toys. She's teething right now so everything she finds she puts in her mouth.

Jacob, 19 - Sophie, 7 months (Lynette, 18)

By the time he's two months old, baby's world is changing rapidly. By three or four months, he sits up with support. Sitting up gives him a much better view of his world. Babies like excitement — their version of excitement. Instead of going to sleep after he eats, he wants to play. Perhaps you'll gently tickle him, move his legs slowly up and down, or give him a variety of objects to hit and grab. He'll enjoy simple games like patty-cake and peek-a-boo.

I tickle Ariana, stand her on my legs, and I have her walk on my legs. I put her on her back and pull her legs up.

Aaron, 17 - Ariana, 6 months (Selena, 16)

Toys for Baby

Her first toys need to be big enough for her to hold easily, yet too big to put in her mouth. Her toys should be washable with no sharp edges or corners. Remove any parts that come off easily. Take out the button eyes on her stuffed animals. By four months, your baby's curiosity is growing fast, and she wants to touch and handle everything possible.

Mom bought Braxton an aquarium, and he sits in front of it. He tries to touch the fish, and he laughs. He makes little Tarzan noises while he watches.

My mom will go "Daddy's here, Daddy's here," and he looks at me with this funny grin.

People say I'm conceited about my son. Of course I am. He's wonderful.

Antonio, 16 - Braxton, 4 months (Susanne, 15)

An inexpensive cradle gym is a good purchase now. It should have simple objects that baby can hit, pull, and handle. If she has a mobile, the best kind is one she can reach, touch, and hit. It needs to be sturdy. Some dads take classes that show them how to make these and other baby toys inexpensively. If you're interested, check with your adult school.

Balls are the best toy of all for baby. She can roll them and throw them. Once she can crawl, she can go after the ball. Soon she'll enjoy a big beach ball as well as having a wonderful time with the smaller ones. Of course she likes it best if you play with her. Even if mom plays with her a lot, your baby needs you, too.

Soft, cuddly dolls and little stuffed animals are important to all children. Most parents now seem to understand boys need dolls as much as girls do. After all, if playing with dolls is early practice toward being a parent, it must be as important for boys as for girls. Most men, as well as most women, will become parents.

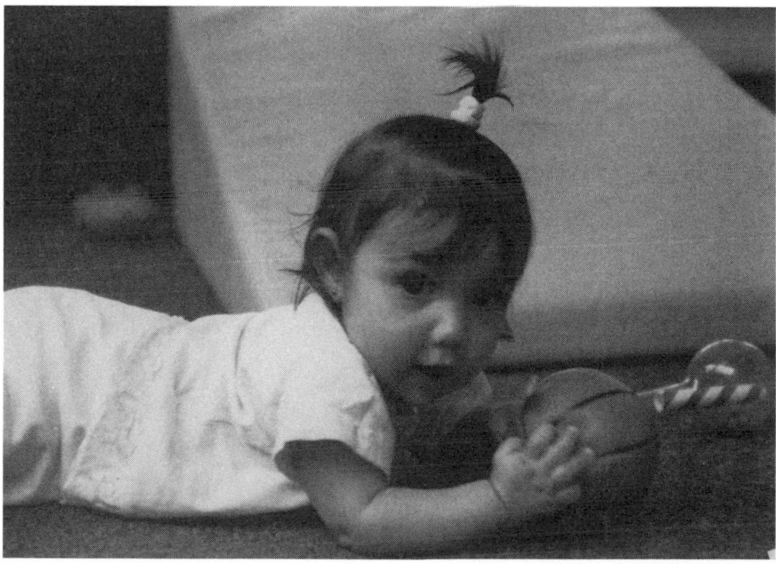

Balls are the best toy of all for baby.

Baby will enjoy going outdoors with you. If she isn't crawling yet, lay her on a blanket near you while you work in your yard. When she starts crawling, let her play on the grass. A little dirt won't hurt her. You need to watch her closely, of course.

We're always outside with her. I wrestle with her, but not hard. I tickle her, move her legs around, dance her around. Her mom reads to her.
Adam, 17 - Brittaney, 10 months (Claudia, 18)

If you have an infant seat, don't overuse it. Your baby would rather be carried in your arms or in a back or chest carrier instead of in a cold plastic seat.

If you're working on your car in nice weather, she may enjoy sitting in her infant seat watching you. Of course you'll put her on the floor or the ground. She is not safe in an infant seat on a table or bench.

As soon as she can sit up by herself, she won't want to sit in her infant seat. By that time, she probably wouldn't be safe in it anyway. She might be able to tip it over.

Build Trust by Responding

It's still important to respond to your baby's cries as promptly as possible. Letting him learn he can trust you to take care of his needs is not going to spoil him. Unhappy, dissatisfied, "spoiled" babies are far more likely to be babies who are already learning they can't depend on dad or mother to come when they need something.

Your baby may be happy much of the time. He giggles and laughs, mimics what you're doing, and generally has a wonderful time throughout much of his day. But he wants you or mom to be nearby.

Crystal smiles and laughs a lot. She growls in the morning like she's mad that people wake her up.

Usually she's real happy. She doesn't cry much at all.

She crawls everywhere. She tries to stand up, bend over, and put something on the table.

Morgan, 17 - Crystal, 9 months (Rebecca, 16)

Baby's Fears

Some babies develop rather strong fears. Sometimes it's the vacuum cleaner. It might be the lawn mower or some other loud noise. She may decide she wants nothing to do with new places or different situations. A trip to the store may upset her.

If the vacuum cleaner frightens her, you could try using it while she sleeps. A better way is to let her look and explore the vacuum cleaner before you turn it on. Then hold her with one arm (lovingly, not scoldingly) while you clean for a few minutes. Don't overdo it, of course, but she may accept the noise under these conditions.

Always, whatever her age, treat your child's fears as the realities they are. It absolutely does not matter if you know "there is nothing to be afraid of." The fact is she is afraid. You need to help her deal with her fear, not scold her.

Stranger Anxiety

By about eight months of age, your friendly baby may suddenly refuse to look at strangers.

Amy really doesn't know my side of the family. When my uncle comes over, she just looks at him. My grandma, Amy looks at her real weird. But she's beginning to get used to grandma now.

Jermaine, 18 - Amy, I year (Angela, 17)

She has matured enough to know exactly whom she trusts. She generally trusts the people she lives with and who take care of her most of the time. Now she doubts the others. Sometimes this is labeled "stranger anxiety."

If you don't see your child regularly and often, you may find he acts as if he doesn't know you. Be patient. Give him time. Let him come to you on his own terms.

She Listens and "Talks"

Sophie says "Da-da-da," but she doesn't say "Ma-ma-ma," and I like it that she said "Da-da" first. When she was first born, I wanted Jacob to be the first to hold her, and he did. I think that's important.

Lynette, 18 - Sophie, 7 months (Jacob, 19)

Your child needs you to help her develop language. You need to talk to her and read to her long before she learns to talk herself. Babies can understand more than you think. They just don't know how to get you to understand their brand of talking.

It's especially important now to talk about the things she knows. As you change her diaper, talk about it. As you dress her, say "Now I'm putting your shoe on your foot. Your hand goes through your sleeve." Name the parts of her body as you bathe her. Talk about the toys you're handing her.

I treat Katherine like a human being. I talk to her constantly. She babbles, and I talk back to her with eye contact. I read to her.

I'd like to go fishing with her.

Paul, 19 - Katherine, 4 months (Kyla, 15)

If you aren't already reading to your baby, start now. Choose very simple stories, preferably with pictures of things she knows. At this age, you may have trouble getting her attention. Reading (mostly looking at pictures) at bedtime is ideal. If she's sleepy, she'll be more willing to sit still for a story. If she sits or lies still long enough for

He loves attention from Dad.

a story, she'll be more likely to go to bed without a lot of commotion.

Curiosity Leads to Crawling

When she started crawling? That was great. The first thing she did was grab her toes and stick out her tongue. When she started crawling, she'd only crawl about a foot. We put our shoes in the middle for a little obstacle course, and she would crawl over them.

Then she learned how to push real hard, and she was gone. She'd get underneath the chairs and hide, or she'd hide in the corner.

Justin, 20 - Niele, 2; Alan, 3 months (Janel, 19)

Your baby's natural curiosity pushes him toward crawling. He'll be delighted when he realizes he can move around by himself. By this time, you need to baby-proof your home.

Put up or away the things he can damage and the things that can hurt him. If baby doesn't live with you, does he visit in your home? If so, you need to child-proof in preparation for his visits.

We child-proofed. We made sure everything was picked up off the floor because babies put everything in their mouths. Nothing that would harm Kevin was left out. Plus when he's that small, you have to be able to see him all the time. You have to keep a constant eye on him. We never leave him alone.

The constant supervision was no big deal. That was some of our best times because I was working part-time and I could stay home with him all day. Now I can't do that.

Zach, 19 - Kevin, 20 months (Erica, 16)

Your baby will learn more if he can crawl freely through your apartment or house. Caging him in a playpen or setting him in his high chair for long periods of time means he's more likely to be bored. When we're bored, we don't learn much. Neither does your baby. Prisons are not for babies. Some experts consider a playpen a baby-level prison.

Sophie is so curious about everything. We don't use a playpen because I don't like them. I feel like if I put my daughter in a playpen, it's like penning up a puppy.

Jacob

Arranging your home so she can freely explore is part of your job as a parent. Baby will appreciate your efforts. The best way to baby-proof is to crawl through your home on your hands and knees as baby will. You'll see things from her level, and you'll realize what you need to put up or away until she's older.

I let Crystal get into things — she gets into the cupboard, but I watch her. If she gets into things, I try to give her something else. She always wanted the phone, but we got her one of her own. That usually satisfies her.

Morgan

Your Baby Starts Teething

The "average" baby (yours may be quite different) cuts her first teeth when she is six or seven months old. For some babies, teething is a painful experience. Others barely notice it. If she hurts, she may want to bite everything in sight. Freeze her teething rings before giving them to her — she'll like them better if they're cold. You can buy teething lotion, which may help soothe painful gums. Put it on her gums a few minutes before feeding time. It may take away some of the pain so she can eat more comfortably.

Right now she's real grouchy because she has four teeth coming out all at once. She already has three on the bottom. When she starts crying, I put gel on her gums. That helps.

Hugo, 16 - Breanna, 9 months (Marcella, 18)

If your baby gets a fever, don't blame it on teething. She may fuss, she may even have a tiny fever if her teeth are bothering her. But if she has a "real" fever (higher than 101°), she's sick. A fever indicates an infection. Call your healthcare provider.

Guard against cavities in those little teeth from the beginning. Encourage her to drink water. It's certainly better for her teeth than are sweet drinks, and water helps rinse milk and other foods out of her mouth.

Avoid sweet foods. During this period you should be able to keep candy and other sweets almost entirely away from baby. If she doesn't know about them, she won't cry for junk foods. The same idea applies to soda and other soft drinks. Don't even give her a taste. Her teeth will thank you.

Nursing Bottle Syndrome

Even a bottle of milk can be a problem for baby's teeth. True, his teeth need lots of calcium to develop properly and to stay healthy. The best source of calcium is milk. He needs about 20 ounces of milk each day at this stage.

When he's old enough to hold his bottle, he may want to take it to bed with him. This is a problem if he keeps the bottle nipple in his mouth as he falls asleep, and it stays there. Milk dribbling into his mouth during the night keeps his teeth covered with a film of milk. Milk, nutritious as it is, has enough natural sugar in it to damage teeth if it stays there hour after hour.

Dentists see so many toddlers with rotten little teeth in front that they have given this condition a name: Nursing Bottle Syndrome.

If baby wants a bottle in bed with her, the solution is to fill the bottle with water. Fruit juice is even worse than milk because it has more sugar in it. If she needs the sucking when she goes to sleep, she can get it with a bottle filled with water or with a pacifier.

Bedtime Routine Is Important

Does your baby have a favorite blanket or stuffed animal? Encourage him to take one special thing to bed with him. Help him find the blanket or teddy bear that is part of the going-to-bed ritual. Read him a story. Then feed him that last bottle of milk as you rock and sing or croon to him. It may take half an hour for him to unwind, to relax enough to go to sleep.

If you follow the same routine with your child every

night, you may find he goes to bed fairly happily most of the time. Your evenings will be more pleasant, too, if putting your child to bed is not a struggle.

Playing Together

She'll love playing with you. Because she likes to imitate, she may enjoy playing follow-the-leader. Keep it simple at first. Clap your hands, put a hat on your head, and wave your arms.

Most children this age love to play outdoors. If you don't have a grassy yard, is there a park nearby? Of course, being outside when you're one year old means lots of supervision from dad, mother, or another caregiver.

Playing is the most important way your baby learns about her world, and remember, you and mom are her first teachers. You can find lots of other ideas for playing with your child in chapters 11 and 14, *Your Baby's First Year*.

An extremely important part of parenting is having fun with your child. *Enjoy her!*

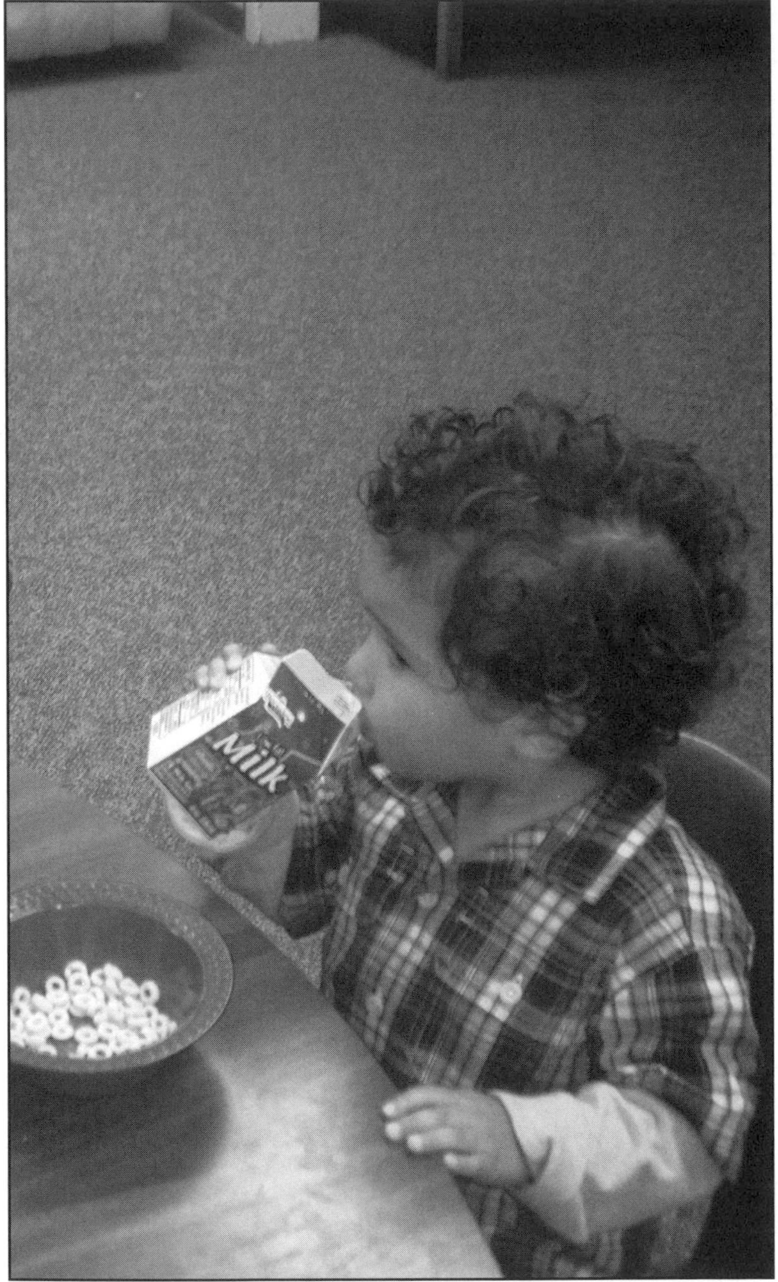

Milk, whole grains, fruits, vegetables, protein keep him healthy.

7

Good Food for Babies and Toddlers

- **Rice cereal first**
- **Vegetables, fruits for baby**
- **She likes to feed herself**
- **Feeding him table food**
- **Not the first year**
- **No junk food**
- **Baby food — read the labels**
- **She can eat with you**
- **Toddlers get picky**
- **You're her model**

Niele eats anything we eat from salads to pizza to ice cream. She loves apples and bananas. We gave her jarred food a few times but once she got teeth, she started eating pretty much what we did. That saved a lot of money.

Justin, 20 - Niele, 2; Alan, 3 months (Janel, 19)

Kianna eats just about everything — hamburgers, Salisbury steak, anything we put in front of her. She stayed on the baby food for about two months. Once we introduced regular table food, she didn't want anything to do with the

baby food. We just chopped regular food up instead of buying junior food. That way she could eat with us.
Daric, 16 - Kianna, 1 year (Kim, 18)

Your baby doesn't need and generally shouldn't have solid food until he is about six months old. Almost all babies get along best on breast milk or formula during this time. If you feed your baby solids too soon, he's more likely:

- to develop food allergies
- to have digestive problems

Don't rush baby into eating solid food. Take your time, and offer only one new food at a time.

Rice Cereal First

It's time to start spoon-feeding about the time she's six months old. Start with infant rice cereal. Use the dry, iron enriched kind that you buy in a box. Rice is less likely to cause allergies than other kinds of cereal such as wheat. Mix the dry rice cereal with a little formula, enough to make it quite thin at first. Use a little spoon — her mouth is little.

Sometimes parents mix cereal and formula together, then feed it to baby from a bottle. Don't! Your baby needs to learn to eat from a spoon.

An infant feeder which practically "injects" the food into her mouth is bad, too. Don't buy it.

Vegetables, Fruits for Baby

She's been eating strained food now for about two months. She wasn't happy about it at first. She didn't like the vegetables so she'd spit it out. She'd move her face so she couldn't eat it. We had a little trouble at first, but now she likes everything.
Jacob, 19 - Sophie, 7 months (Lynette, 18)

Perhaps Jacob started feeding Sophie solid food a little early. If your baby doesn't like the solid food at first, wait a week or two, then try again.

Start feeding baby vegetables, fruits, and their juices sometime between his fifth and seventh months. Mashed banana is often one of the first foods given to baby. Most babies like it, and it's super-easy to mash to a smooth consistency.

At first, offer baby only one new food each week. If he's allergic to that food — if he gets a rash or seems to have a digestion problem — you'll know that particular food is probably causing the problem. If you fed him a new food each day, you wouldn't have any idea which one you needed to remove.

She Likes to Feed Herself

When we feed her she grabs the spoon and tries to hold it. We give her a few cheerios so she'll leave us alone while we eat. If we give her a baby cookie, she wants the whole bag.

Jacob

Your baby can probably:

- Hold and gum a teething biscuit by six months.
- Handle little pieces of hard-boiled egg yolk (no egg white yet) by six months.
- Eat dry unsugared cereal, soft toast, French toast, cooked carrot and potato pieces, peas with skins broken, even diced liverwurst sandwiches by seven months.

She can eat all these things herself by using her fingers. Unsweetened Cheerios are a marvelous early food-toy. She'll pick one up in each hand, look at it, stick it in her mouth. They contain some nutrition and, most important, are very low in sugar. Don't give her sugar cereals. Such "cereals" should be labeled breakfast candy. Some are more than half sugar!

Feeding Him Table Food

Brittaney eats a lot. She eats baby food and lots of fruit, noodles, fresh fruit. Her mom smashes the fruit, then cooks and blends it. We don't put salt in her food. It's not healthy for babies.

Adam, 17 - Brittaney, 10 months (Claudia, 18)

If you wait until he's six months old to start baby on solid food, you'll need to use strained food for only a couple of months. He can be eating table food, much of it mashed, by the time he's eight months old. In fact, you won't need to buy jars of junior food. Feeding him from the family meals is better for baby.

He's eating about everything we eat. He likes fruits, apples and pears. We cook them and mash them up. We chop up the chicken real fine for him. Of course he drinks milk.

Tony, 16 - Felipe, 16 months (Alicia, 17)

Mash his food into small pieces. If you're serving chicken, get rid of the bone and cartilage. Then cut the meat into very small pieces for him.

She hates baby food now. She eats it very rarely. We started giving her table food at ten months – peas, cabbage, carrots, fruit. We started giving her meat when she first got teeth. We give her fish and ground beef. She loves ground beef. She eats when we eat plus in-between we give her baby snacks.

Jermaine, 18 - Amy, I year (Angela, 17)

Fish is excellent because it just falls apart. Of course, you have to be very careful to get all the bones out first.

> **Warning**
> Orange juice is not recommended until baby is about a year old. Some babies are allergic to it.

Many babies like cottage cheese. Just mash it with a fork.

Plain unflavored yogurt is good for baby. Don't choose the heavily sugared kind. Many children prefer the tart flavor of plain yogurt.

The above foods, along with breast milk or formula, can supply most of baby's vitamin and mineral needs. Iron fortified cereal can satisfy his need for iron. Fruits and vegetables, of course, are good sources of vitamins A and C. Your doctor may also want baby to take vitamin drops.

Not the First Year

Raw, crisp fruits and vegetables aren't good for baby until past the first year because he might choke on them. In fact, until he's two, if you want him to have raw carrots, you should grate them.

When he's five or six months old, offer baby a little breast milk, formula, or juice in a cup. You can buy a cup with a lid and a spout as a bridge between bottle and cup. Before long, he'll be able to drink a little formula, water, and juice from his cup.

Now is the time to help your baby grow into a pattern of healthy eating that will continue throughout his life. Feeding him a variety of foods gives him an opportunity to develop a taste for different foods.

No Junk Food

If you don't see your child often, you may want to take her candy, cola, or other junk food when you visit. Don't!

Sometimes people try to pacify a child with a sweet

treat when a hug would work just as well. In fact, hugs are always better than junk food. Jello water and other sweetened drinks are in the empty calorie category too.

We don't give her cookies much, and we don't give her soda. Very little sweets, because my mom told me my cousin got a lot of sweets, and her teeth all decayed. Our doctor told us baby's teeth are real soft.

Jason, 17 - Melanie, 13 months (Heather, 17)

Babies and toddlers need milk, water, and unsweetened fruit juices to drink — and seldom anything else. Coffee, tea, and cola drinks contain caffeine, which is a drug. Your baby doesn't need drugs.

We give Ashley little pieces of apple and orange, oatmeal, cereal with me in the morning. She eats pretty much what we eat.

Danny, 18 - Ashley, 15 months; Aaron, 3 weeks (Disiree, 16)

You'll do her a real favor if you delay giving her junk food — soda, candy, chips, etc. — as long as possible. Your job is to help her learn to enjoy eating the food she needs to grow into a healthy, capable adult.

Baby Food — Read the Labels

If you decide to buy strained baby food, read the labels carefully before you buy:

- Choose basic fruits, vegetables, and strained meats.
- Don't buy combination meals because you get less protein per serving with them than if you mix together a jar of meat and a jar of vegetables yourself.
- If the label tells you the food contains a lot of sugar and modified starches, don't buy it.
- Skip the baby desserts because baby doesn't need sweet desserts any more than the rest of us do.

She Can Eat With You

If you're frying food for your family, it's better for your toddler if you broil or dry-fry her food in a non-stick pan. Serve her food before you add the spices or the rich sauce. Foods to avoid completely at this age include popcorn and nuts or any food that might cause her to choke.

> *He's not real picky. We eat at 6 or 7 p.m., and he eats with us. He lets us know when he's done, and we let him down.*
>
> *He has sweets maybe once a week. I ate a lot of sweets when I was a kid, and your teeth suffer and your body starts to suffer. I started getting heavy and lazy. I don't want him to go through that.*
>
> Jarrod, 19 - Wade, 18 months (Valerie, 17)

Give her small helpings of food. Don't worry if she doesn't seem to eat much during the months after her first birthday. She doesn't need as much as she did six months ago when she was growing so much faster than she is now. She needs daily:

- twenty ounces of milk
- fruits and vegetables
- bread and cereal
- protein foods

If she doesn't drink enough milk, put it in puddings and soups. Does she like cheese? Let cheese take the place of some of her milk. Cottage cheese and yogurt are also good replacements.

Allow plenty of time for your toddler to eat. Rushing through a meal is not her style. She'll eat many foods with her fingers, but by her second birthday, she'll be able to handle a spoon quite well.

She'll be messy while she's eating. She may rub the food into her hair and all over her face. She'll drop some on the floor. You can put a big plastic garbage bag or a thick layer of newspaper under her chair to catch the spills.

Toddlers Get Picky

Deziree is picky. If we aren't eating something, she won't eat it. She has a few nights where she'll eat two things off her plate, then get down and play. We usually try to feed her something before she goes to bed, like a bowl of cereal.

Parnell, 18 - Deziree, 18 months (April, 20)

Most toddlers go through stages when they're very picky about their food. He may eat only a few foods. It's okay to have a limited diet as long as it's balanced. Encourage him to eat something each day from each of the basic food groups — fruits, vegetables, milk, whole grains, and protein foods (meat, poultry, fish, dried beans and peas, cheese).

Don't try to force or even coax him to eat. Offer small servings of nutritious food. Don't offer sweets at all. If he seems to need an in-between-meal snack, make it part of his daily food plan.

If he doesn't want to eat any lunch at all, calmly take his food away. He won't starve by suppertime. Just don't tide him over with a handful of cookies an hour later.

If he eats all his food and asks for more, give it to him in the same way, without an emotional reaction. Eating all his food is not what makes him a "good boy."

Children who are offered nutritious food and very little junk food tend to eat when they're hungry. If they aren't hungry, they probably shouldn't eat anyway. So don't nag! Instead, offer him the good food he needs, then use mealtime to talk about what's happening today.

A toddler needs some structure at meal time. He should be fed at about the same times each day. He also needs a comfortable place to eat that is suitable for his small size.

He should remain seated until he's through eating, and then be allowed to leave. Most toddlers will eat better with some companionship. However, they should not have to sit and wait for other people to complete their meal.

You're Her Model

Mark and Kelly Ellen were eating a lot of junk food. When they realized that Dustin was copying their poor food habits, they decided to change their ways. Mark explained:

> *For three or four months Dustin had cola all the time. He'd go through all the sodas. The same with Twinkies and cakes. We were drinking a lot of cola and had potato chips everywhere.*
>
> *Then we realized all that junk food was getting expensive and we were both gaining weight, so we started a little diet. Now we don't even buy sodas. Now we're real conscious about what we eat, and the same goes for him. For the last year or so, we won't give him junk food. We learned from experience. If he has candy all day, he gets higher and crankier.*
>
> *Junk food is like a lot of other things. If it's there and it's annoying, just take it away. As you take it away, explain why he can't have it. If we had a box full of cakes and cookies, he'd be into it. So we stopped having junk in the house.*
>
> Mark, 22 - Dustin, 21/2 (Kelly Ellen, 20)

Your modeling is all important in the development of your toddler's food habits. If you're a picky eater, or if you survive mostly on junk food, you can expect your child to do the same thing. If you're careful to eat foods from **MyPyramid** groups at each meal, your child is more likely to eat well, too. When this happens, payoff is high in terms of your toddler's health and general development. Her disposition is likely to be better, too, because she'll feel better if she eats the foods she needs.

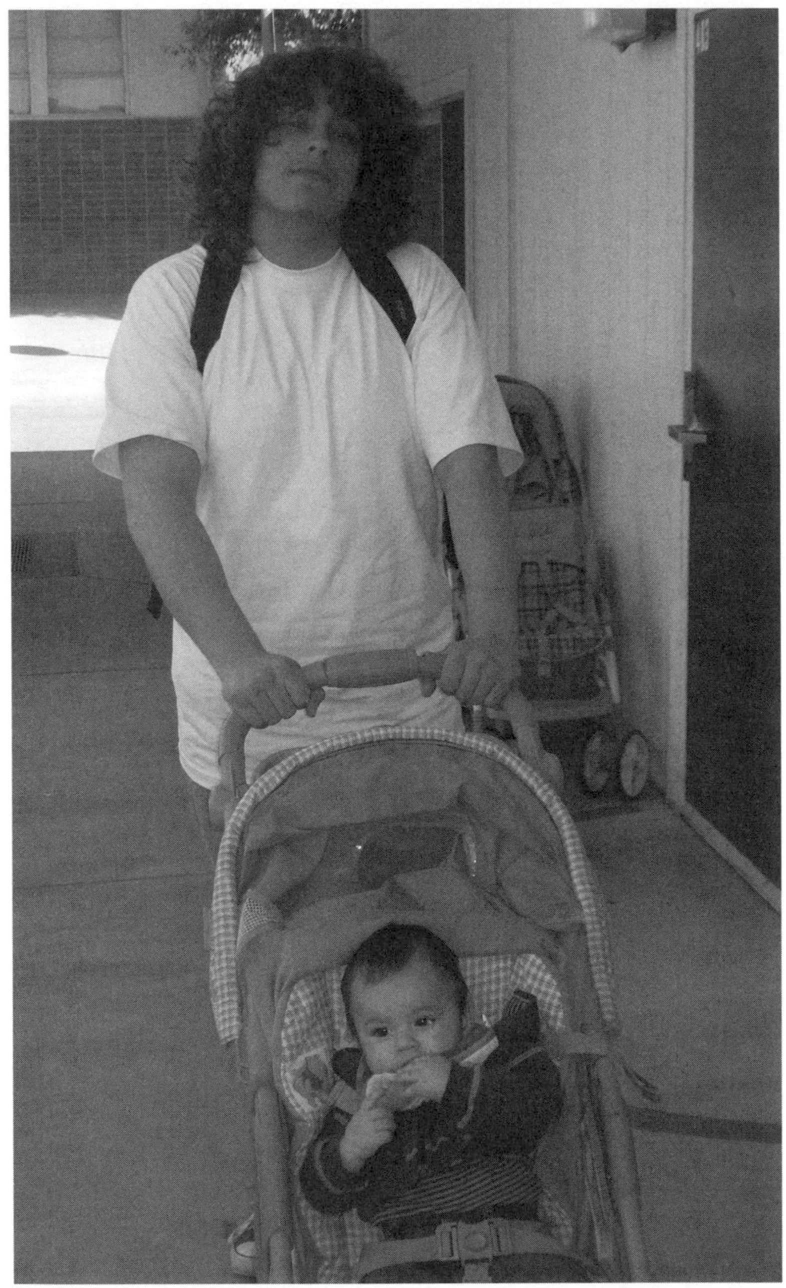

Keeping him safe and healthy is a big responsibility.

8

Health and Safety for Your Child

- **When to call doctor?**
- **Dealing with fever**
- **Diarrhea can be serious**
- **Colds are common**
- **Smoke can cause infection**
- **Importance of immunizations**
- **Possible reaction to shots**
- **Accident-proofing home**
- **Start with the kitchen**
- **Other hazards**
- **Accident-proof outside areas**
- **Poisoning is big danger**
- **Is paint lead-free?**
- **Health and safety — an important challenge**

Deziree's been sick more than half the winter — ear infections and bronchitis. She had to go into the hospital six times for bronchial infections.

One time she got pneumonia and had to get tubes in her ears. She's been good through most of it. We can tell if her ears hurt because she plays with them. Now, with the tubes, they drain.

Usually she runs a fever when she doesn't feel good. When it gets too high, we take her to the doctor.

Parnell, 18 - Deziree, 18 months (April, 20)

Kolleen had gas so bad she'd cry real hard for ten minutes straight. I'd give her to Leanne, and when she got frustrated, she'd give her to my mom.

Holding Kolleen real tight helped. Wrapping her in a receiving blanket and walking around the house, or giving her a pacifier, or going outside in the fresh air helped.

Everybody says you got to let her cry. It's like we can't — if she gets used to it, she might cry more.
Santos, 17 - Kolleen, 17 months; Jameka, 5 months (Leanne, 16)

When Should You Call Baby's Doctor?

- Baby has a temperature above 101°. Most doctors want a call if baby's fever gets this high, but check with your doctor. When does s/he want to hear from you?
- Baby gets a rash.
- Baby vomits most of his meal. Many babies spit up occasionally during the first two months, and it's not a problem. But if baby, after every feeding, suddenly vomits most of his meal, call your healthcare provider immediately.
- Baby has diarrhea for 12 hours.
- Baby indicates ear pain, usually by tugging at his ear and/or crying.

When these things happen, call your healthcare provider, but don't panic.

Karina has asthma, and she came close to dying twice. Usually we could tell when she was getting it. No matter what, I never got real scared because when you get scared, you panic. If you panic, you can't help your kid. You have to be calm and take care of her. Myndee would freak out, and if we both panicked, we couldn't do anything. We'd try to give Karina her medicine, and keep her comfortable until we got her to the doctor.

Luis, 20 - Benito, 8 months; Karina, 3 years (Myndee, 21)

Before you call your doctor, make some notes about your baby's condition. Then you'll be able to describe his symptoms more accurately:

- Is he coughing? For how long?
- Has he lost his appetite?
- Does he have diarrhea?
- What is his temperature?
- Has he been exposed to any diseases?
- Has he received all of the immunizations he should have had by this time?

If your doctor prescribes medication for your baby, ask if you should give baby all the medicine in the bottle, or should you give it only for a certain number of days?

Dealing with Fever

Fever is one of the early signs of illness in a baby, and you shouldn't ignore it. There are many devices available for taking baby's temperature. Ask the baby's healthcare provider which one they like best. When you call the doctor, include information about which device you used.

What can you do about fever at home? Give the baby Tylenol® or other non-aspirin pain reliever as recommended by your doctor.

Cooling baths are another way to bring fever down. If baby shivers while you're bathing her, it's too cold. A good way to do this is to put a towel in lukewarm water. Then wrap the baby in the wet towel. It helps bring her temperature down, and she's less likely to shiver.

Lukewarm water is the best thing to use. Don't use alcohol. The fumes can be dangerous for baby to breathe.

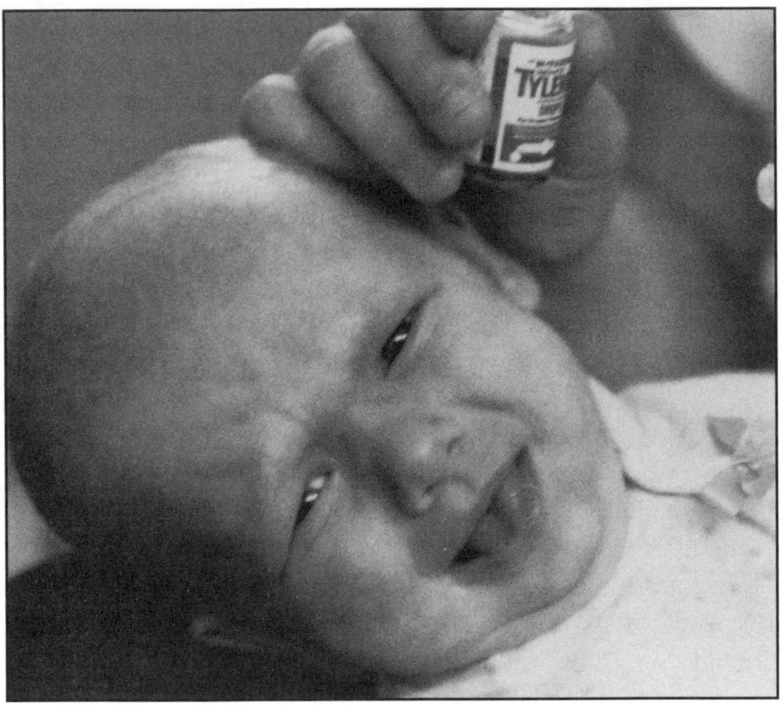

The doctor may suggest Tylenol® if baby has a fever.

It's also important to give your child liquids when she has a fever. If it's a sore throat that's causing her fever, she may not want to do a lot of sucking. When this happens, offer her a popsicle. It will provide some liquid.

> *He's had quite a few ear infections. He's always playing with his ears. Once he starts pulling at his ears, we know something is wrong. When he's sick, he isn't himself. He's miserable no matter what you do.*
> Jarrod, 19 - Wade, 18 months (Valerie, 17)

When your child has an ear infection, call the doctor. While a non-aspirin pain reliever can take away some of the pain and the fever, it doesn't kill the germs causing the infection in the ear. Only prescription medication can do that, so you need to take baby to the doctor. There's a real danger of permanent hearing loss if an ear infection is not treated promptly.

She's been sick a few times. A couple of times we took her to the doctor because she had an earache. They gave her medicine — and said it was because of the bottle. They said when we laid her down with her bottle, the milk could go to her ears. We don't do that now.

Adam, 17 - Brittaney, 10 months (Claudia, 18)

As discussed in Chapter 5, many infants' ear infections are caused by propped bottles.

Diarrhea Can Be Serious

Diarrhea: *a thin, watery, foul-smelling discharge.*

If baby has this condition for as long as twelve hours, call the doctor. A baby with diarrhea can quickly lose a dangerous amount of fluid.

Treat diarrhea by giving the baby clear liquids and nothing else for 24 hours. Liquids you can give him include Pedialyte® (non-prescription liquid you buy in the drugstore or grocery store), clear water, or water mixed with apple juice (one tablespoon apple juice to 8 ounces water). Offer no solid foods, but feed liquids as often as he'll take them.

Colds Are Common

He's had one cold. If he's sick, he wants to be held. We do it, it don't matter what has to be done, dishes or make dinner, it's more important to hold him.

Jarrod

Neither you nor your doctor can "cure" your child's cold — there is no known cure. You *can* help him be more

comfortable. If he has a fever or headache, Tylenol®
may help.

Ariana's had a stuffy nose like twice, and she hates when you touch her nose. When it was runny, we put salt water (normal saline) up her nose and gave her Tylenol®. After awhile she got better.

We try not to take her out when she's sick.

Aaron, 17 - Ariana, 6 months (Selena, 16)

If she has a runny or stuffy nose, use normal saline and a rubber syringe to clean the discharge from her nose. Normal saline is available from the drugstore without a prescription. The hospital probably gave you a rubber syringe for this purpose for baby.

Decongestant medicine may also make her feel better. If her nose is sore, cream or ointment on the area is soothing. If she's coughing, your doctor may recommend cough medicine. If she has a stuffy nose, a cold-water vaporizer will help her breathe more easily. The old-fashioned steam vaporizers are dangerous, and they don't work as well.

If she doesn't want to eat, don't worry. When she's feeling better, she'll be hungry again. Encourage her to drink juice, water, clear soups, even a little weak tea.

How often your child has a cold depends on two things: the number of people with colds to whom she is exposed, and her own resistance. If she's in good health generally, eats nutritious meals instead of junk foods, and gets plenty of rest, she is much less likely to get sick.

Smoke Can Cause Infection

Alexis had an upper respiratory infection. We took her to the doctor, and he gave her medicine.

I'm a smoker. I don't smoke around Alexis, but the doctor said she can pick it up from my car or my clothes. I mostly smoke at work because it keeps me calm. When I come home, I change my clothes.

She's had it twice now, the upper respiratory infection. A lot of my friends are smokers, and she's around them, too.

Dennis, 17 - Alexis, 6 months (Tara, 20)

Your child may be sick more often if someone smokes around him. Research clearly shows the dangers of second-hand smoke. Some people find it extremely difficult to stop or cut back on their smoking. If someone in your family smokes, is s/he willing to smoke outside rather than in the house? Your child is likely to feel better in a smoke-free home.

He's been sick with lots of coughing and allergies. We use the vaporizer, and if that don't work, we take him over to the doctor.

Hilario, 16 - Cesar, 9 months (Guadalupe, 15)

A stuffy nose can also be caused by an allergy. Doctors usually recommend changes in diet for babies with allergy symptoms. Some allergies are caused by plants, animals, or pollutants. Often, a baby's allergy symptoms disappear as he grows older.

Importance of Immunizations

Some illnesses you can prevent. Children used to die from diphtheria, whooping cough, polio, and other "child-hood" diseases, Now you don't have to worry about these illnesses. Just make sure your child gets the DTaP and other immunizations (shots) he needs. These are recommended by the American Academy of Pediatrics:

- **Hepatitis B** is given in a series of three injections. Usually the first is given on baby's first day after birth, the second at one to two months, and the last one at six months. Baby must have all three.

- **Diphtheria, Tetanus, Pertussis (DTaP)** is also given in a series of three at two, four, and six months with a booster (Td) between 15 and 18 months.
- **H. influenzae, type b (Hib)** is another series of three. This is often given in the same injection as the DTaP and is then called HDTaP.
- **Rotavirus (Rv)** is a new vaccine that prevents diarrheal diseases. It is given at two, four, and six months.
- **Pneumococcal** prevents a type of pneumonia common with young infants. It is given at 2, 4, and 6 months.
- **Polio (IPV)** is a red liquid given by mouth or injection at two and four months. A third dose is given between six and 18 months.
- **Measles, mumps and rubella (MMR)** is given once at 12-15 months. A booster is given at 4-6 years.
- **Varicella (chickenpox)** is given once at 12-15 months.
- A skin test for **tuberculosis** is usually given at 12-15 months, often at the same time the MMR is given.

While this may seem like a lot for baby, it is important to remember that all of these diseases can cause death or very serious illness in children. *Don't take a chance with your baby!*

It is also *very important* to keep a record of your child's immunizations. *If you lose it, get another one right away.* When your child starts school, the school will insist on having this information. It may be hard to get it several years later.

Immunizations are free at the health department. They may be given by the health department at local parks. If you don't know where to take your baby for his shots, ask your school nurse for a recommendation.

Possible Reaction to Shots

When Sophie had her shots she cried hysterically. She didn't want to stop. The last time she went to the doctor she was shaking her head, "No, no." I've only gone once with them because I'm usually at work. Plus I couldn't see my baby start crying. I'd probably want to hurt the doctor!

Jacob, 19 - Sophie, 7 months (Lynette, 18)

Most babies have some reaction to immunizations. Usually the reaction lasts only a day or two and is mild. Giving your child a baby non-aspirin pain reliever such as Tylenol® (or whatever your healthcare provider recommends) will help relieve these symptoms.

Of course, if your baby has a severe reaction to his immunizations (high fever for more than twelve hours or other severe symptoms), you should call your doctor.

He may need extra rocking after he's had his shots.

Accident-Proofing Your Home

Wade grabbed hold of a hot curling iron last week. Every morning now when Valerie does her hair, we have to make sure we put everything back up in the cabinet so he can't get to it.

I smoke, and for awhile he was trying to grab a lit cigarette. He runs around like a nut, and he'll fly face first into the rocks, but the curling iron was the worst.

Jarrod

Accident-proofing your home is absolutely essential if you have a baby, toddler, or preschooler living there. If your child doesn't live with you but is in your home occasionally, it's still extremely important that your place is safe for him.

Accidents injure and kill many young children every year. In fact, accidents are by far the greatest cause of injury and death for this age group — thousands are crippled for life or killed annually.

Start with the Kitchen

At my house sometimes I leave the skillet handle facing out, and I'll have to change that. I'll have to put things in the sockets and check out the kitchen. If they're going to move in with me, I have to make it safe. When I lived by myself, it didn't matter.

Darrance, 17 - Jaysay, I year (Victoria, 17)

The kitchen is a marvelous learning laboratory for babies and toddlers. Designing it so it's safe for your baby is an important challenge. Hazards in many kitchens include:

- cleaning supplies (Don't keep them in the cupboard under your sink.)
- knives
- vegetable grater

- ice pick
- cooking fork
- hot pans (Keep the handles turned toward the back of the stove.)
- coffee pot, toaster, and other appliance cords
- iron and ironing board
- gas stove with controls baby can reach

When your child has a minor accident such as touching the stove and burning his fingers slightly, help him understand what happened. Don't say anything about "the bad stove" burning him, and don't fix it up with cookies. Sympathize, of course, but also explain that if he touches the stove when it's hot, he'll be burned.

If you ever smell gas in your home, phone the gas company at once. In most areas, they send someone out to check it at no charge to you.

Other Hazards

Water is one of the leading causes of death for children under 3. Also, babies who swallow too much chlorinated pool water sometimes suffer convulsions later.

If you live near a pool, be sure the gate is securely closed at all times so that toddlers cannot get into the area.

Another danger for the child is the baby walker. If a baby in a walker falls down steps or tumbles into a pool, results may be deadly — much more dangerous than if he falls freely. In fact, a number of states passed legislation banning baby walkers because of these risks.

If there is a cloth or placemat on the table, your pulling-to-stand baby will grab it. Anything setting on the cloth, whether it's hot coffee or an empty dish, is likely to be pulled down with disastrous results for your baby.

A thin plastic bag, the kind that dry-cleaners use, can

suffocate a baby if she pulls it over her face. Cut up and throw out such bags immediately.

During the time she is pulling herself to stand, be especially careful to keep the bathroom door closed. It's possible for a toddler to pull herself up by the edge of the toilet, lose her balance, fall in, and drown.

> *We put locks on the cabinet that has all the chemicals. We keep the bathroom door closed all the time.*
>
> *Deziree gets it open sometimes now, but usually the doorknob is loud enough so we can hear her going in. We also get up and check on her when she's too quiet.*
>
> Parnell

Put all medicines in a cabinet and keep that cabinet securely locked.

If you have a fireplace, open heater, heating register, or

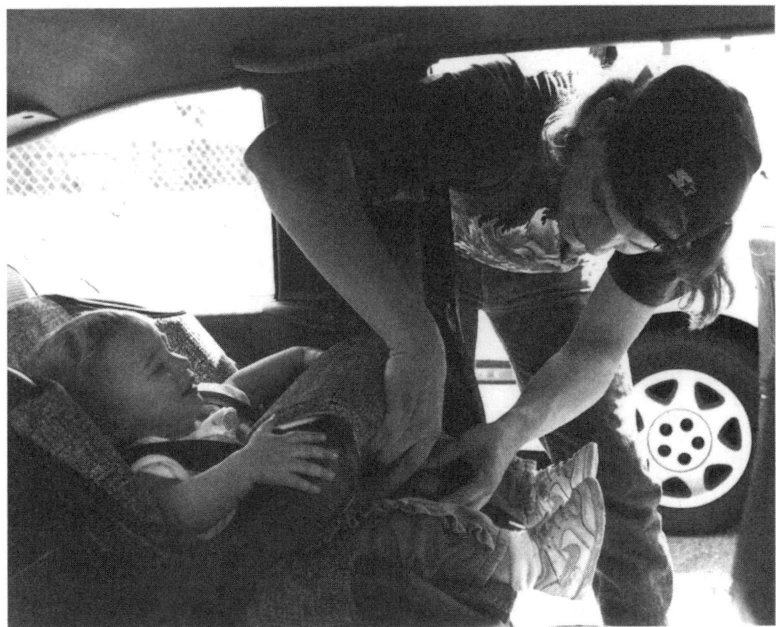

Buckle him in securely – he depends on you for his safety.

floor furnace, put guards in front of and over it. Use furniture to block off radiators.

If your toddler has learned to open doors, you can attach fasteners, the hook-and-eye kind, up too high for her to reach. You'll need some method of keeping doors closed if they lead to stairways, driveways, and some storage areas.

Burke is much more active now. He has a swimming move, trying to crawl for a little, then stop, look at you, then try to crawl again. Or he'll get frustrated or just lay his head down to rest.

When he starts crawling, I'll have to put the gate on the stairs, keep him away from the stove, etc.

Shane, 16 - Burke, 61/2 months (Jumana, 15)

If you have stairs at your home, put a gate at the top and bottom to protect your creeping-crawling-toddling child.

Your window and door screens should be securely fastened. If your house has bars on the windows, they need to be the kind that can be opened from the inside.

Cars can be deadly for toddlers. If he's in the car, make sure he's buckled into his car seat. If he weighs 60 pounds or more, he can use the regular seat belt. (Weight varies from state to state.) Incidentally, be just as sure that you're buckled in, too. You're his model.

Accident-Proof Outside Areas

Yards, fenced or not, and garages need to be childproofed, too. Check for:

- trash
- insecticides
- paint removers
- other poisons
- nails, screws, and other hardware
- assorted car parts, tools, and gardening equipment

Get rid of the trash. Store the other things out of reach or lock them in the garage.

Also get rid of rusty or tippy furniture. Regularly check hammocks, swings, and other play equipment for safety.

Some plants are poisonous such as caster beans and oleander. Does your yard have shrubbery or other plants dangerous to your child? Also check any house plants in your home. Some philodendron and dieffenbachia are toxic. So are the bulbs of daffodil and other bulb plants.

Poisoning Is Big Danger

Children are most likely to be poisoned when they're ten to twenty months old. By this age, they move around a lot, explore everything in reach, put everything possible in their mouths. They aren't able to understand what's dangerous and what's not.

Cigarettes are poisonous. If members of your family smoke, ask them to keep ash trays away from your toddler.

Find the telephone number of your nearest poison control center. Keep it by your phone along with your healthcare provider's and other emergency numbers. If you think your child has been poisoned, take any evidence you have of what he swallowed — a piece of the substance or its container.

Get some syrup of ipecac from your pharmacist and use it if your healthcare provider or poison control center recommends it. It will help your child throw up. For some poisons, this is appropriate.

For others, such as toilet and drain cleaners, it's exactly what you don't want. Throwing up Drano® will cause twice the damage because the lye burns going down and again coming up.

Is Paint Lead-Free?

Do you have furniture, walls, or woodwork in your home that were painted before 1970? If the paint contains lead, it can damage your child if he chews on the painted surface. If the paint is peeling, he may put bits of it in his mouth. Lead poisoning can be the result, a serious problem for babies and children.

> *Aviantay had to go to the doctor because she ate some paint and got lead poisoning. Her mother had to get another house because the paint was chipping off the walls. Monique caught it at the right time, but it really scared her. She called me and told me Aviantay was in the hospital for a day. She's all right now.*
>
> Lorenzo, 17 - Aviantay, 2 years (Monique, 18)

If children get too much lead, they show signs of lead poisoning. "Too much" for a baby may be a very little bit of the paint. The child may become anemic and lose his appetite. He may be either listless or hyperactive and irritable. He may find it harder to learn, and may suffer convulsions and permanent brain damage from the poisoning.

If you suspect lead poisoning, check with your doctor. Through a simple blood test, s/he can detect the condition. If lead poisoning has occurred, the doctor can recommend treatment to get rid of much of the extra lead in your child's body so he won't have the problems described above.

Health and Safety — An Important Challenge

Keeping your child safe and healthy during her toddler years is an important part of your parenting career. It's up to you and her mother to create a safe environment for her. It's up to both of you to care for her when she's ill.

It's also up to both of you to guide her toward eating the good foods and getting the rest she needs for optimal health. As you already know, parenting provides lots of challenges.

Your reward for meeting these challenges is your child's well-being and love.

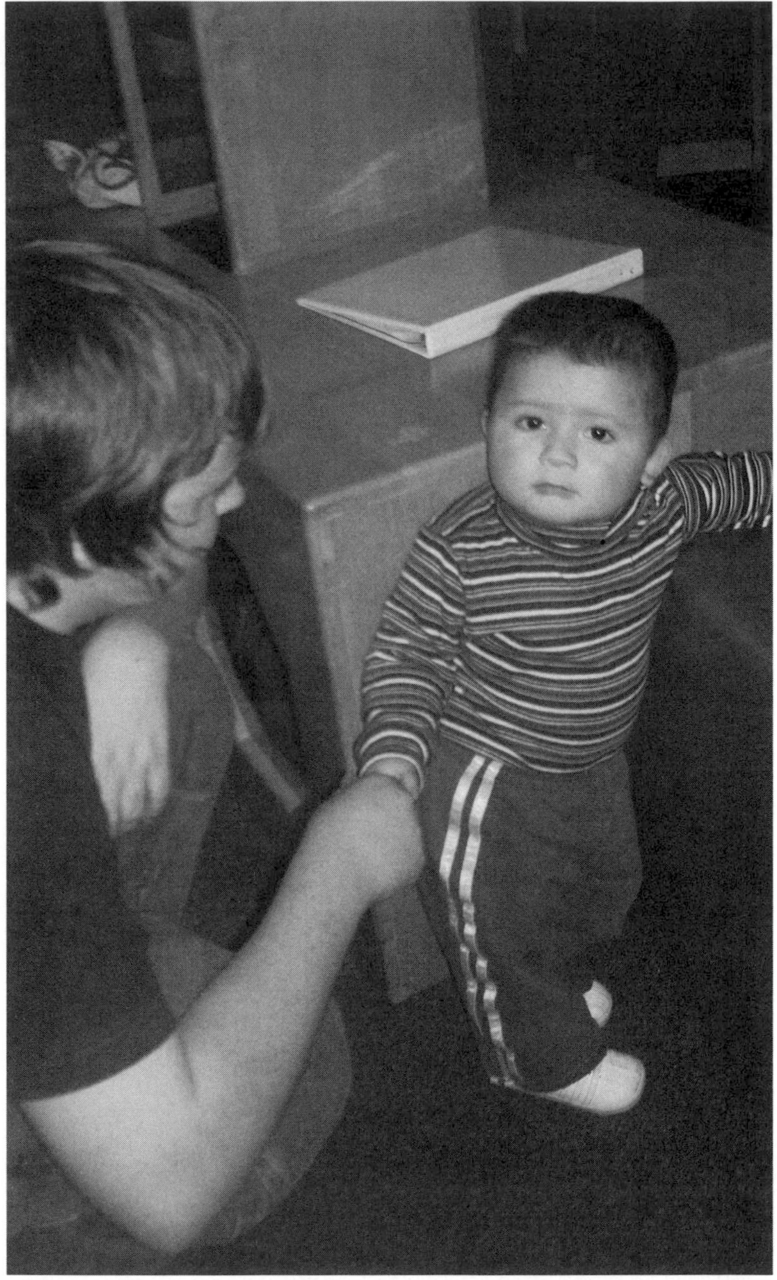

He's learning lots of new things — and will be running soon.

9

She's One — Soon She'll Be Running

- **He develops rapidly**
- **She copies Dad and Mom**
- **He struggles for independence**
- **Dealing with temper tantrums**
- **When he asks for help**
- **Don't rush toilet teaching**
- **Helping him talk**
- **Read — read — read**
- **Bedtime ritual**
- **Every-five-minutes routine**
- **Tips on weaning**
- **She keeps you busy!**

Lily's smart — she imitates everything we do. If we read to her, she grabs the book and starts mumbling stuff. If we feed her, she wants the spoon even though she can't feed herself yet.

Marco, 18 - Lily, 1 yr. (Serene, 18)

Now that she's a year old, Amy pulls everything off the table — a lot of stress. But regardless of what she do, that's what babies are. They get into a lot of stuff.

When she started crawling, we put childproof latches on the cupboard doors, and gates by all the stairs and doors. We put her toys on the floor so she can get to them.

We put those plastic things in the sockets, and we try to keep the cords high. We're always watching her, too. She tries to get into everything.

Jermaine, 18 - Amy, 1 (Angela, 17)

I like the way Valizette laughs and tries to talk. That's what kept me thinking when I was doing my thing on the streets, I can't do that. I can't get killed or go to jail because I have a baby.

Jamal, 16 - Valizette, 16 months (Shawnté, 17)

He Develops Rapidly

During his first year, your child develops from a helpless newborn to a whirlwind little person who scoots everywhere and will be walking soon. He can climb, and he can get into big trouble if no one is watching him.

My mom has those little glass things like porcelain dolls and flowers all over the place, and Roman gets into all that stuff.

The bathroom door is always closed because he plays in the water in the toilet.

The other day I found him on top of my computer desk. He was knocking everything off. It was funny — but how did he get up there?

We keep putting breakable things higher and higher but Roman keeps getting higher and higher. He stands on his little choo-choo train and climbs up on things. He doesn't walk yet, but he climbs everywhere.

Jimmy, 17 - Roman, 1 (Rosalva, 19)

A one-year-old likes toys — form boards, blocks, balls, and stacking toys. He especially likes these toys if someone is there to watch or to play with him. Already he enjoys crayons or paints if he's allowed to use them.

Deziree loves to scribble. She likes finger paints, markers, and colored pencils. I didn't think she'd be learning this fast. She gets a learning toy, and she figures it out within a week.

Parnell, 18 - Deziree, 18 months (April, 20)

He's starting to talk through words and gestures. He can follow simple directions. His understanding of right and wrong, however, won't begin to develop until he's close to two. Even then he often won't know or understand what he should and shouldn't do.

She Copies Dad and Mom

Your toddler loves to copy you. If you're working on your car, she'll want to help. Does she have a little car to work on with you?

When I work on my truck, he climbs under the truck and gets full of grease and dirt. He tries to fix everything. If I'm working on something here in the trailer, he'll grab a screwdriver and try to help me.

He does just about everything I do. If I throw one of his balls, he'll throw it. If I go out the door, he'll go out the door. He pretty much follows me.

Jarrod, 19 - Wade, 18 months (Valerie, 17)

When you're working in the house, there will be lots of opportunities for her to mimic you. If you don't mind some water on the floor, and if you use plastic dishes, you can let her wash dishes with you. Cooking with dad or mom is exciting for your toddler. Can she help stir cookie mix and drop spoonfuls on the cookie sheet?

If you copy her movements and her play activities, she will be delighted. Letting her know you like what she's doing is the best way to help your child have high self-esteem. This is an important part of her learning.

He Struggles for Independence

Amber wants what she wants when she wants it. I pretty much try to change her attitude, get her attention elsewhere. If it's something simple and won't hurt her, I give her what she wants.

She doesn't want any help, not even with her eating. She's always been independent.

Zaid, 19 - Amber, 15 months (Tiffany, 20)

Your toddler wants to feel in control of what he eats, the clothes he wears, when/whether he uses the bathroom, and how he plays. Give him plenty of chances to make some of these decisions. If you do, he may find it easier to go along with your wishes when you can't let him choose.

Compromise and respect are magic ingredients for living with a toddler. Being sensitive to your child's need to control some aspects of his life will help you understand his behavior. When your toddler was an infant, it was your job and his mother's job to decide what was best for him. As he grows, he will insist more and more on making his own decisions. His individuality and independence will amaze you.

Elena's very independent. Sometimes it scares me. At this age, I wonder how she'll be when she's a teenager.

When she started this, it got my attention. I would sit there and think, "Oh my god. "I would go in her room, and she would literally grab me by the hand and lead me out, then close the door.

Or she would get mad at us and go in and close the door because she wanted to be alone. I guess that's okay. Her room is a safe place, and I can understand wanting to be alone. Sometimes I feel that way.

Carlos, 19 - Elena, 23 months (Monica, 18)

Dealing with Temper Tantrums

Toddlers tend to get frustrated because they can't express themselves in words very well. Temper tantrums may result. She wants to put her clothes on herself, but it's a struggle. She tries to put a square block in a round hole and it doesn't work. And she probably doesn't want your help. She has these frustrations, and she can't talk them out. She doesn't know enough words yet so she screams. Her screaming may turn into a real out-of-control temper tantrum.

When Merlalcia has a tantrum, I put her on the floor on the carpet where she can't get hurt. I leave her until she calms down, and then I talk to her, "That's not a good thing to do." Then she gives me a hug and says, "I love you."

I try to manage my time to talk to her, read to her,

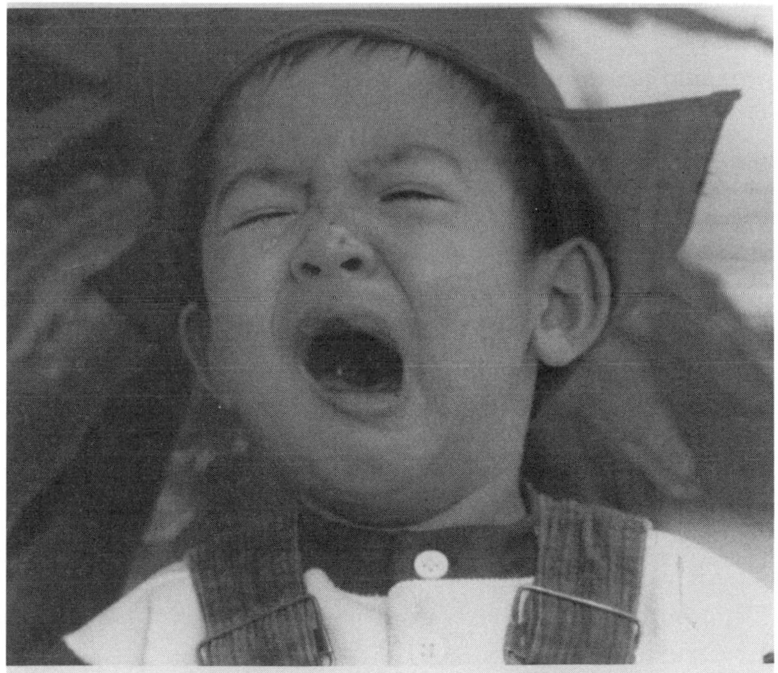

He isn't enjoying his tantrum any more than you are.

and play with her. When she cools down after a tantrum, I start playing with her.

Khusba, 22 - Merlalcia, 11/2 yr. (Aurora, 17)

The tantrum is an expression of her feelings of anger and frustration and her inability to cope. Her feelings are sincere and strong. She is enraged and absolutely miserable. She has lost control of her behavior and may be very difficult to handle.

Losing control in this way can be scary for her. She wants to do things her way. At the same time, she needs your firm guidance. What should you do?

First, what should you not do? Don't spank or otherwise punish your already-upset child. If she's having a "real" tantrum, she's lost control of her own actions. If she's "just" screaming, hitting her won't help, and it usually won't stop her screaming.

Don't give in to her either. Is she screaming because you said she couldn't have a cookie right before dinner? Don't stop the screaming by handing her a cookie. If you do, what happens next time? She screams when she wants another cookie. She learns that's the way to get that cookie.

Shaquille has a temper. He starts yelling, and I hold him until he calms down. Some people don't understand that hitting them doesn't resolve anything. When you hit them they aren't learning anything. When you talk to them, explain to them, they listen, and probably won't do that again.

Lester, 17 – Shaquille, 16 months (Traci, 16)

It may be best to ignore a temper tantrum. You could pick her up calmly and take her to her room, but if she's lost control, you probably don't want to leave her alone.

An even better approach may be holding her gently. Feeling the security of your arms may have a calming effect. She isn't enjoying her tantrum any more than you are. After all, she is a very upset little child, and she needs to know you still love her — even though you won't give in to her demands.

> *Genevieve has tantrums over the car keys. She'll have my keys, and I'll say I have to go, and I take them. She'll throw herself down and start screaming. I think I'll buy her a keyholder with fake keys that will look like my Bart Simpson holder.*
>
> Miguel, 20 - Genevieve, 18 months (Maurine, 16)

Miguel is wise to figure out a way to eliminate the cause of Genevieve's tantrums. See *Discipline from Birth to Three* (Lindsay and McCullough) for more discussion of this topic.

When Your Child Asks for Help

Responding when your child asks for help is the best way to cut down on the number of tantrums he will have:

- When your child wants you, stop to see what he wants.
- If possible, provide the help he needs.
- At your child's level of understanding, briefly talk about the event.
- Once you have assisted or comforted and talked to your child, your next step is to leave him alone.

Your child learns a lot from an interchange like this:

- He learns to use another person (you) as a resource when he can't handle a situation himself.
- He learns that someone thinks his discomfort, excitement, or problem is important, which means he is important.
- His language development also gets a boost each time this happens.

Don't Rush Toilet Teaching

Toilet teaching is not appropriate for most children under two. They simply are not ready. Trying to teach him to use the toilet too soon only frustrates parent and child.

See the next chapter for suggestions on how to teach your child to use the toilet when he's ready.

Helping Him Talk

Chanté is talking a little — "Move," "Mama," "Dada," "Can I have joo?" We read to her.
Tiger, 19 – Chanté,18 months (Crystal, 18)

How can you help your child learn to talk? You already are, *if* you talk to him a lot. And you're helping him even more if you're reading to him.

Are there words you don't want him to say? Then try not to have those words said where he can hear them. He learns words by hearing them, and this applies to "bad" words, too. To him, all words are interesting, and if you scold him for saying certain words, he'll have no idea why. If he says words you don't like, it's usually best to ignore them.

There are two other ways you can help him:

- Don't correct his speech, and don't talk baby talk to him. He needs to hear words spoken correctly. He'll learn faster if you don't criticize him if he mispronounces a word.
- Give him a chance to talk. If he points at the refrigerator, don't pour him a glass of juice immediately. Encourage him to say the word. Don't frustrate him, of course, by waiting more than a few seconds. Remember that children start talking at different ages.

If you speak two languages, help your child learn both. It might be best if one parent or caregiver always speaks one language to him, and the other parent or caregiver speaks the second language. This may help your child keep the two languages separate. By the time he enters kindergarten, he should speak both languages well.

Read — Read — Read

I've always read to him, ever since he was tiny. He'd look at the pages when he was a month old. He was fascinated with it. Now he loves his books. "Book, book," he'll say.

He says, "Me read," and he makes noises.

Zach, 19 - Kevin, 20 months (Erica, 16)

If you've been reading to your child, she probably is talking more than she would have otherwise.

Choose books with bright simple pictures for your toddler. At first, she'll prefer pictures of familiar things, cats and dogs, for example.

As she grows older, of course, you won't limit her books to stories about familiar things. The rhythm of Mother Goose rhymes will appeal to her. Fairy tales and stories about animals, people, and places she has never seen are an important part of her education. Provide lots of variety in her books, because books can widen her knowledge of and interest in many different things. Books about familiar topics, however, are more likely to keep a toddler's interest.

Develop a Bedtime Ritual

Bedtime is Amber's worst thing. She gets cranky when she's tired. She doesn't want anything, and she knows we want her to go to sleep. She'll do anything to avoid it. If we try to rock her to sleep, she rubs her eyes or pulls her ear to keep herself awake. She never wants to sleep because she doesn't want to miss any of the exciting stuff. She finally goes to sleep about 10 p.m., but she wakes up a couple of times each night.

Zaid

She needs her rest because she's so active.

Toddlers are extremely active, and they get very tired. Many resist napping. Waiting until he's exhausted before putting him to bed is not a good plan. He'll be less cranky if he eats and rests at regular times.

If he doesn't want to nap in the afternoon, let him take some books and a quiet toy to bed with him. Tell him it's okay if he doesn't go to sleep, but that you want him to play quietly for an hour. Some days he may go to sleep, and other times he won't. Whichever, his quiet hour will refresh him for the rest of the day — and you, too!

A baby who went to bed willingly his first year may suddenly turn into a toddler who insists on staying up. By now, he enjoys being with his parents and doesn't want to leave them. When he hits the "No" stage, bedtime may become a problem.

It's important that your child have a regular bedtime. You can't keep him up until 10 tonight, then expect him to lie down and go to sleep at 8 o'clock tomorrow night.

Starting a bedtime routine when the child is six to eight months old usually helps him settle down to sleep without a lot of fussing. At this age, it's probably as simple as holding him while he drinks his bottle, reading him a story, and putting him in his crib.

A few months later, a more complicated ritual can help prevent bedtime problems. Quiet play, a little snack, a relaxing bath, and reading help prepare a toddler for sleep.

The important part of the ritual is carrying it out regularly. If you or mom can't be with him some nights, his caregiver needs to carry out his usual bedtime ritual.

If your child is hungry at bedtime, give him a light snack or a bottle before he goes to bed. Then brush his teeth. If he still needs something to suck on as he drifts off to sleep, give him a bottle of water or a pacifier. Either will satisfy his urge to suck.

Every-Five-Minutes Routine

If you haven't started a bedtime routine, try it. If your child continues to have a fit when you put her to bed, think about the reasons. Is it as simple as a dislike of the dark? A night light might help.

Probably she doesn't want to be alone. She may feel deserted if you put her in bed, tell her to go to sleep, then shut her door.

If she cries and you get her up, guess what? She'll cry tomorrow night until you get her up again.

If you decide to let her cry, she may go to sleep in a few minutes. Some toddlers, however, will cry and cry for a couple of hours if left alone. They may finally go to sleep from exhaustion, but they aren't likely to sleep well after such an ordeal.

Combining the two methods (leaving her alone and giving her attention) might work. If she makes a big fuss at bedtime, explain (again) that it's time for her to go to bed. Tell her you'll be in the next room. Pat her back for a minute, tell her "Goodnight," and walk out.

If she cries, go back five minutes later, explain kindly that it's time for her to go to sleep, pat her back and say "Goodnight" again, then walk out. Repeat the process every five minutes until she finally goes to sleep.

She might cry for another hour the first night, but she knows you haven't deserted her. She knows you still love her. She also knows she is to stay in bed.

For the toddler who's been getting up or staying up at night, it may take a week or so to adapt to a regular bedtime. When she does, she's likely to be a happier child because she's getting the sleep she needs.

By the time your child is a year old, she doesn't need milk in the middle of the night. If she gets a bottle at bedtime, she doesn't need more food. If she sleeps with a bottle of milk in her mouth, the risk of tooth decay is high.

If she wakes, instead of handing her a bottle, offer her a cup of water. Tell her "Good night," and walk away. If she continues crying, try the every-five-minutes routine for a week. You'll be exhausted, but if she starts sleeping through the night, you'll feel better, too, next week.

Weaning from the Bottle or Mom's Breast

You've probably been encouraging your child to drink milk, juice, and water from a cup for several months now. If she has plenty of time to learn to drink from a cup, weaning from the bottle or mom's breast is likely to go more smoothly.

Drinking from a cup is quite different from sucking fluid from a bottle. She might like to use a cup with a drinking spout at first. Transferring to a cup later won't be difficult.

For some children, giving up the bottle is hard. Some

people believe it's easier for the child (and dad and mom) if she switches from bottle to cup soon after she's a year old. She may be less willing to change if she's been sucking from her bottle for two years or more. On the other hand, some children seem to need more sucking than others.

Two things need to happen when you decide it's time to wean her from the bottle:

- She has to get enough milk — or enough calcium from other sources such as yogurt and cottage cheese.
- You and mom need to be comfortable that she's telling you she doesn't need the sucking experience any longer.

With encouragement from you and her mother, your baby may practically wean herself from breast or bottle.

She Keeps You Busy!

Chanté gets into everything. She opens drawers, doors to the outside, dumps things out of drawers. We tell her "No," but she doesn't pay much attention.

Tiger

During her second year, your child will keep you and/or her mom busier than you ever dreamed possible. You're most likely to enjoy her if you:

- Design her surroundings so she can have as much freedom as possible.
- Give her the attention she craves.
- Set truly necessary limits, and insist she not go beyond those limits.

Good parenting is indeed an art. Your child will give you lots of opportunities to practice this art during her second year. *Enjoy!*

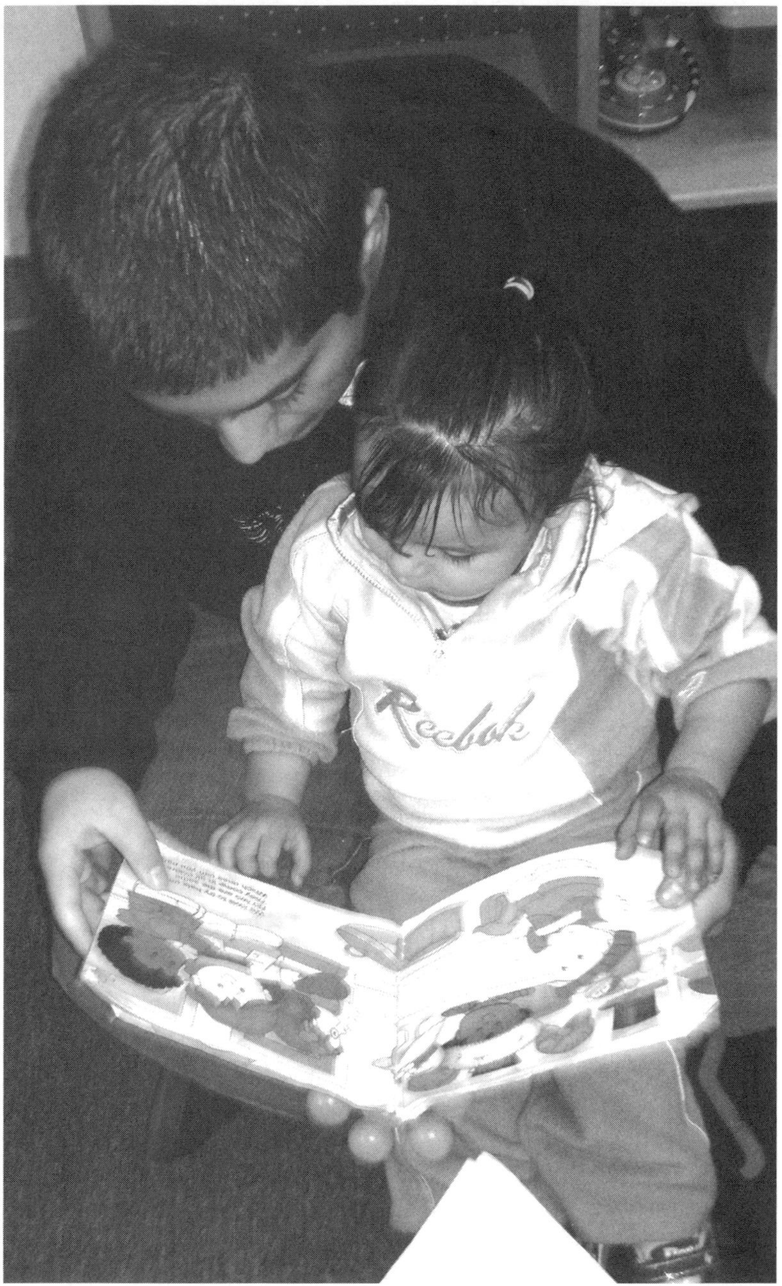

She loves to have Dad read to her.

10

Your Amazing Two-Year-Old

- **Plan painting time**
- **How much television?**
- **Playing outside**
- **How much rough-housing?**
- **"Where do babies come from?"**
- **Father-child time**
- **What about toilet-teaching?**
- **Punishment doesn't help**
- **If you live apart**
- **Your toddler's amazing world**

Now that Chamique is older, almost 2, she speaks in full sentences and she speaks clearly. She even says "Please" and "Thank you."

Tim, 20 - Chamique, 21 months (Jocelyn, 19)

When I come home from work and I'm tired and this little voice says, "Daddy," sometimes it brings tears to my eyes. It brings a whole new dimension to life, feelings and experiences you'll never have until you're a father. It's different, and it's real neat.

Zach, 19 - Kevin, 20 months (Erica, 16)

"No" was one of her first words. She's very talkative. She puts on her pants and her socks herself. She knows how to open doors, turn on the TV, change the channel.

When she does things, we clap. She's always alert, wanting to do new things. We sing songs like "Three Little Monkeys."

She has one of those jeeps, and I take her outside to ride it. I take her all over the house with her on my back, playing horsey.

Lucas, 21 - Kamie, 21 months (Kelsey, 19)

By the time your child reaches two, he's running, jumping, and riding wheel toys. He helps dress and undress himself, and feeds himself with a little help. He enjoys coloring and painting. He will continue to imitate your activities and those of others. He'll imitate activities you like as well as some you don't. Simple playthings often are more inviting to a toddler than elaborate toys.

If you buy a new TV, or, better yet, a big appliance such as a range, save the box for your toddler. Help him make a house out of his box. You can also throw a blanket over a card table and tell him he can play in his cave.

Plan Painting Time

Provide plenty of opportunities for your toddler to color, paint, cut paper (with blunt-ended scissors), and do other creative activities. You'll continue to supervise, of course.

Take a tip from preschool teachers and do a little organizing of your child's day. Plan a time when she can finger-paint or paint with a brush. If the weather permits, painting outside cuts back on clean-up time.

It's best not to give your toddler a coloring book in which she's expected to color or paint between the lines. If she's at all creative, she'll have a much better time with big pieces of paper on which she can scribble as she wishes.

Let your child use whichever hand she prefers. If she's left-handed, you'll probably know by the time she's three.

How Much Television?

Research shows that aggressive children tend to watch a lot of violence on television. Research also shows that children who watch too much TV show less imagination in play and at school than do children who see less television.

A toddler who watches TV for several hours each day is missing the active play he needs. He's also undoubtedly watching shows with scary scenes, shows that give a distorted view of relationships between men and women, and other situations that tend to scare or confuse him.

> *We don't want Elena watching horror films. In fact, I don't think a child should watch that much TV. It's not good for their development.*
>
> *There's too much violence, and it can pollute their minds.*
>
> Carlos, 19 - Elena, 23 months (Monica, 18)

Can you watch TV with your child and talk with him about what he sees and hears? If you two watch an hour or so of carefully selected shows a day, and talk together about it, TV may have a positive influence on your toddler.

If your family watches a lot of TV, you may have little choice in the number of hours the set is on each day. Probably the best tactic in this case is to find a quiet place where you and your child can play away from TV.

Playing Outside

Toddlers enjoy playing outside. It's good for them. They are usually more active outside than inside. The exercise helps their motor development. It also gives them a better appetite and makes them more ready for bedtime.

I saw Karina yesterday. We go crazy. We wrestle. We go to the park, and we went to Disneyland last month. I've taught her how to swim.
Luis, 20 - Benito, 8 months; Karina, 3 years (Myndee, 21)

Do you have a fenced-in yard where your toddler can play? If so, she — and you — are lucky. Of course she'll still need lots of supervision.

If you don't have a yard, can you take her to a nearby park? She'll also enjoy going for a walk with you. It won't be the kind of walk where you get lots of exercise from walking fast. Your toddler will be in no hurry. Instead, she'll explore all sorts of things along the way.

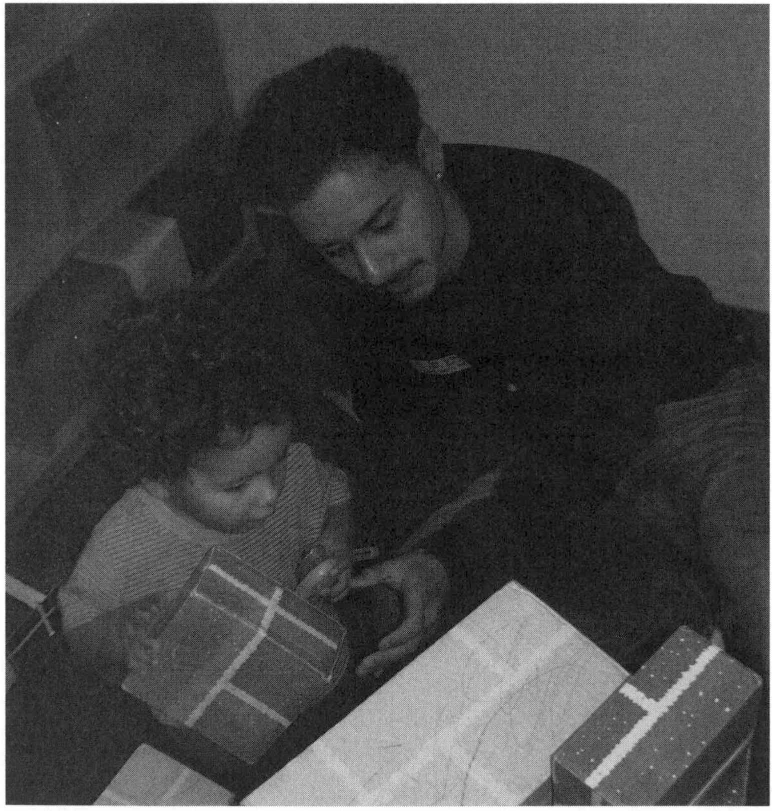

Playing with big blocks with Dad is exciting.

Every other day in the summer we take Leah to the park. There's a lake down the road, and we go for walks in the park and watch the ducks fly.

In the winter we go to another lake to see the ducks.

Lyle, 19 - Leah, 30 months (Lyra, 18)

Giving your child a lot of new experiences helps her learn about her world. Take her to the airport to watch the planes landing and taking off, to the train station, and to a construction site. She'll have a great time, and these are things you can do together whether or not you live with your child.

How Much Rough-Housing?

Rough-housing is an activity that toddlers and parents, especially dads, often enjoy. It's not smart, however, to play at hitting each other if you don't want your child to hit other children. Neither is it wise to get your child so excited that he'll have trouble calming down.

I think parents set the pace. My husband likes to play rough. Then he gets tired and wants to stop, but the kids aren't ready to stop. You can't just all of a sudden stop. You have to start going slower and taking it easier. It took him awhile to learn that.

Annabel, 26 - Andrew, 10; Anthony, 7; Bianca, 5; Brooke, 2

Active play usually is not a good idea at bedtime. You want your child to slow down. That's why a bedtime routine including a story time works best.

"Where Do Babies Come From?"

Your toddler may start asking questions about sex. If he does, let him know you appreciate his questions, then answer in terms he can understand. When he asks, "Where do babies come from?" you might say, "Babies grow in a special place in the mother's body."

If he asks how the baby got inside the mother, you can tell him that a mother and a father make a baby together. You might explain that the father's sperm gets into the mother through the father's penis.

Sometimes little girls wonder why they have no penis, and little boys worry that their penis might come off. Explain that boys and girls are made differently. Teach your child the correct names for his/her genitals. Name them as you name other body parts.

All little boys and girls handle their genitals. When they do, and find that this feels good, they may masturbate. This does no harm. It is normal, and you would be wise to ignore it.

A parent who tells his child that masturbation is bad may cause the child to feel naughty, or to think that sex or sexual feelings are bad. That's not a very realistic or healthy approach.

Father-Child Time

I feel a father should be involved because your child is only young once. Once they grow up, you can never ever get that back. You should spend as much time with them as you possibly can. By doing that, you see your child progressing, and you don't miss out on her life.

My family is more important than anything else in my life. My job can come and go, but every year my child gets older, and I will never get that back.

Me and Elena, we have our time together. I try to spend as much time with her as possible. But sometimes when I'm working, I'm exhausted when I get home. She will run around and say, "Daddy, daddy," and I'll sit there comatose. But I like to play with her, and she likes it, too, or I read her a story. She loves books.

Carlos

You're probably tired when you come home from work. You may have little energy left for playing with your child. However, most children look forward to a special playtime with their dad. When this happens, a bond develops between father and child that brings pleasure to both.

This bond is the best possible basis for good discipline. If you don't live with your child, it's even more important to plan special times with him.

What About Toilet Teaching?

Toilet teaching should seldom be considered for children under two. Most children aren't ready to use the toilet until after their second birthday. Some are quite a bit older. Attempts at early toilet teaching must seem strange to a child.

Imagine you're a toddler. Your parents put diapers on you for months. They change them when you get them wet or messy. Then one day they put another kind of panty on you, and suddenly it's an "accident" if you get those panties wet or dirty. Confusing.

You'll save yourself and your child a lot of frustration if you cheerfully diaper her until she decides she wants to use the bathroom.

Actually, successful toilet teaching depends much more on development than guidance. She won't be able to urinate or defecate reliably in a potty chair or toilet until she can recognize her need to go.

She also needs to develop some control of the muscles that control the release of urine and BM (feces). Training her to sit on a potty chair before she's ready is quite meaningless, a waste of time for both of you.

Punishment Doesn't Help

Don't punish your child for accidents. Toilet teaching can't be forced. A child who feels pressured will be tense and unable to urinate when he chooses. He will be even more likely to have accidents.

When your child has an accident, calmly clean it up and put clean clothes on him. He has not misbehaved; it was an accident, and he should not feel ashamed.

When he is successful, praise him. Tell him how happy you are that he was able to do that. It will help if other family members let him know they're proud of him, too.

The ideal way to teach your child how to use the toilet is through modeling. You show him how. If you encourage your child to sit on his little potty chair while you're on the big toilet, he'll get the idea faster.

Even after teaching has been going quite well, some children start having frequent accidents again. If this happens to your child, don't be concerned. Handle the accidents calmly. If they occur too often, you may need to put diapers on him until he seems ready to try using the toilet or potty chair again.

Some children learn quite easily while others have a more difficult time. Because every child is different, there is no one sure method or any particular age that is best for all children. Your child will learn to use the toilet when he's ready.

If your child spends much time in a daycare center, or with grandma or another caregiver, it's important that you all work together with him when he's ready to go to the toilet.

If You Live Apart

If you aren't living with your child, do you see her often? Always be sure, if you tell her you'll be over tomorrow, that you are there when you said you'd be there. Sometimes single mothers complain that their child's dad doesn't show up when he promised he'd be there. This can be very disappointing to a child.

Children need to be able to trust both parents. Trust goes away when the parent says s/he will do something with the child, then doesn't carry through on that promise.

If your child's mother doesn't want you to see your child, what can you do? Unless the court says otherwise, you should have the right to spend time with your child. Perhaps if you're dependable in your visiting — let her know when you're coming, and always follow through with your plans to spend time with your child — she will cooperate.

> *I go over there every week. Every other week I bring Erica home for the weekend. I talk with her, and I play with her. I read little books to her when she goes to bed, and she goes to sleep. I sit there with her for awhile to make sure she doesn't wake up. I like to take her to the park and walk around with her. I take her other places, too.*
>
> Larry, 19 - Erica, 6 months (Priscilla, 17)

Your Toddler's Amazing World

The whole world is fantastic to your toddler. Everything is new. Toddlers really don't need Disneyland because they can find excitement wherever they are.

Your job is to share his excitement, and to guide and support him as he discovers his world.

Discipline (teaching) without harsh punishment works best with babies and toddlers.

11

Guiding Your Child Through Discipline

- **She wants to please you**
- **Sharing childrearing beliefs**
- **She's learning rapidly**
- **Setting limits**
- **She learns by exploring**
- **Making it easy to behave**
- **Shaken infant syndrome**
- **Toddlers and discipline**
- **Being yelled at hurts him**
- **Must children be hit, slapped, or spanked?**
- **Punishment interferes with learning**
- **Child abuse happens**
- **Helping your toddler behave**
- **Discipline strategies**

I don't spank her. I just talk to her. I guess she can tell by the tone of my voice. I got child abuse, and I'm not going to touch my kid. I try to be a better parent than my mom was.

I take care of her and talk to her and let her know by my mouth, not put my hands on her.

I know how much I didn't like being hit. I got put out when I was 14. Right now I'm kind of violent at times, and I feel she don't deserve something like that.

Lorenzo, 17 - Aviantay, 2 years (Monique, 18)

When I was younger, I was hit a lot. I don't ever want to hit my son. I want him to have the respect where he knows I'm disciplining him by word of mouth. I don't want to use physical force — I don't think it's right. I was beaten and it didn't help me. It just built into my anger and made me more violent.

Todd, 18 - Avery, 6 months (Celia, 19)

He went through the "No" stage pretty early — from the time he was about a year old. It's rough. He stands there and he says "No." Sometimes it makes me pretty angry. We can't yell at him because he really doesn't know what he's saying.

I'm surprised that we don't do much spanking. Usually when we talk to him, he listens. We let him play with a lot of things, but we watch him, and he knows there is a limit.

Jarrod, 19 - Wade, 18 months (Valerie, 17)

What do you think of when you say "discipline"? Punishment? Discipline means to educate. It comes from the same root as disciple, one who is taught. In this sense, your child is your disciple. It's your job to guide and teach your child to behave in ways that will help him cope with the world he lives in.

Your teaching will help him have a more satisfying life, both now as a child, and later as an adult. You can discipline your child best in a child-safe place with interesting things to explore and to use for play. The most important part of discipline is making it easy for children to behave correctly.

When I was growing up, my dad wasn't there, he was in prison. My mom used to say, "You're punished," and five minutes later I'd be out, and I'd break a neighbor's window. She would smack us when we were little, but when I got older I'd say, "You can't hit me."

It's kind of like how you're raised, what you do, but you know what, I'm really learning how to do it the opposite.

All the stuff we don't want Kolleen to get we put higher than she can reach. She can do whatever she wants with all the stuff in her room.

We have these things on drawers so she can't open them. We discipline her, but we don't spank her or yell at her. She knows when I tell her "No." She has a sad look, and she knows.

Santos, 17 – Kolleen, 17 months; Jameka, 5 months (Leanne, 16)

She Wants to Please You

She's not two yet, and already she likes to please us. When I'm stern with her, and I'm pretty big, she listens. Whether or not she does what I say, she knows something is wrong.

Two thoughts on this — I try not to overdo it because if you do, it loses its effect. The other thing is that for the most part we're real nice to her, and she likes us and she likes being with us. When I say something stern, it matters to her.

John, 21 - Mandi, 22 months (Danielle, 20)

Most of the time discipline is not a difficult task. Your child by nature wants to please you. Usually she will try to behave the way she thinks you expect her to behave.

Her natural curiosity and her drive to explore will cause problems at times. All children need some help to control or limit undesirable behavior. A caring relationship built on love and trust makes it easier for your child to accept limits on behavior.

Sharing Childrearing Beliefs

You and your partner need to share with each other your ideas on childrearing, especially in regard to discipline. Most parents have strong feelings about how a child should be handled.

If one parent has been brought up by parents who spanked a lot and the other wasn't, it may be hard for them to agree on discipline methods for their child. It's important that everyone who interacts with your child agree as much as possible on discipline (learning) techniques.

She's Learning Rapidly

Your two- to three-year-old is busily learning new words and is more able to talk. She usually understands what you tell her if you use simple words and short phrases. There will be many times, however, when she doesn't interpret the meaning correctly. To her, words generally have very simple meanings and uses. She has just barely begun to learn about language.

Now that she's older, she's started touching a lot of things. We've childproofed stuff – fixed cupboard doors so she can't open them. We also put little rubber things on the corners of the tables, and put covers on the outlets.

The dog's food and water were on the floor in the kitchen. When she started crawling, she'd go for the food, so we had to move that.

Tim, 20 - Chamique, 21 months (Jocelyn, 19)

Often when a toddler seems to behave defiantly, she simply doesn't understand how she's expected to act. You can help her if, before speaking to her, you stoop down and get eye contact with her. Now you have her attention. Talk to her slowly and use words you know she understands.

She'll learn faster if she feels secure in your love.

Setting Limits

You'll have to set some limits. A child who always does whatever he feels like doing whenever he wants to do it is likely to cause problems for himself and others. Since limits cut back on his freedom to explore and learn, however, set as few as possible.

Once you've set a limit, stick with it. Being consistent is extremely important. Your limits define safe play areas and play things. Your limits provide a sense of security because he knows what he can do. He knows that someone is watching and caring.

He will learn about limits through discipline. Note, the word is discipline, not punishment. Punishment should not be a part of disciplining babies and toddlers.

She Learns by Exploring

At first, you'll need most of the discipline yourself. It is you who must stop the wrong behavior.

If she puts something dangerous or dirty in her mouth, it's up to you to take it out. Objects not to be touched must be out of her reach. You need to move her away from unsafe areas, or you need to set up barriers.

Alexis was beginning to get into stuff, and she'd make me mad. I'd keep telling her, "Don't do this, don't do that." I would yell at her a lot, but I'm trying not to yell so much now.

I need to put stuff up where she can't reach it. If I don't do that, I have to watch her a lot, because otherwise she'd crawl away and get something else.

Dennis, 17 - Alexis, 6 months (Tara, 20)

Once she starts creeping or crawling, you will have a problem if your home is not child-proofed. She wants and needs to explore. That's how she learns.

Making It Easy to Behave

Babies don't understand what they should or should not do. They simply must explore because that's where they are in their development. Slapping his hands when he reaches for things isn't likely to change his behavior. It can damage his trust in you and make future discipline more difficult. Make it easy for him to behave. If you don't want him to touch something, put it away!

If he wants something he can't have, and it can't be put out of reach, you must take responsibility for keeping him away from it.

> *We're going to keep stuff off the tables so we won't have to say "No" all the time. Julie's mom has a coffee table with little coasters, flowers, stuff like that. We're talking to her about moving all that stuff away from the living room and the kitchen. She's willing.*
>
> Jason, 18 - Josh, 3 months (Julie, 17)

If you're unwilling or unable to child-proof your home, you must be willing and able to spend an enormous amount of time helping your child cope with his surroundings. Eventually, of course, your child will learn that some things are his and some are not. Some things can be played with and others can't. This may not happen until he's nearly three or even older.

Shaken Infant Syndrome

Sometimes a parent shakes an infant or child who is misbehaving. This is a physically dangerous thing to do.

An infant's neck is quite weak. At first she can't even hold up her head. The head of an infant or even a child is large and heavy compared to the rest of her body. If she is shaken, her head will bounce back and forth between her back and her chest. She's not yet able to stiffen her neck muscles to protect it.

At this young age, her brain is smaller than the skull. This allows room for the rapid growth of her brain. Therefore, if her head is shaken, her brain will be tossed around within her skull. Her brain may become bruised and swollen. The shaking may cause some bleeding and blood clots as well. It can result in permanent brain damage or even death.

While many children will appear to survive a shaking without any handicap at all, they may not be as intelligent as they otherwise would have been. Problems with vision or learning may also appear later.

Even throwing a baby up in the air in play is not safe for these same reasons.

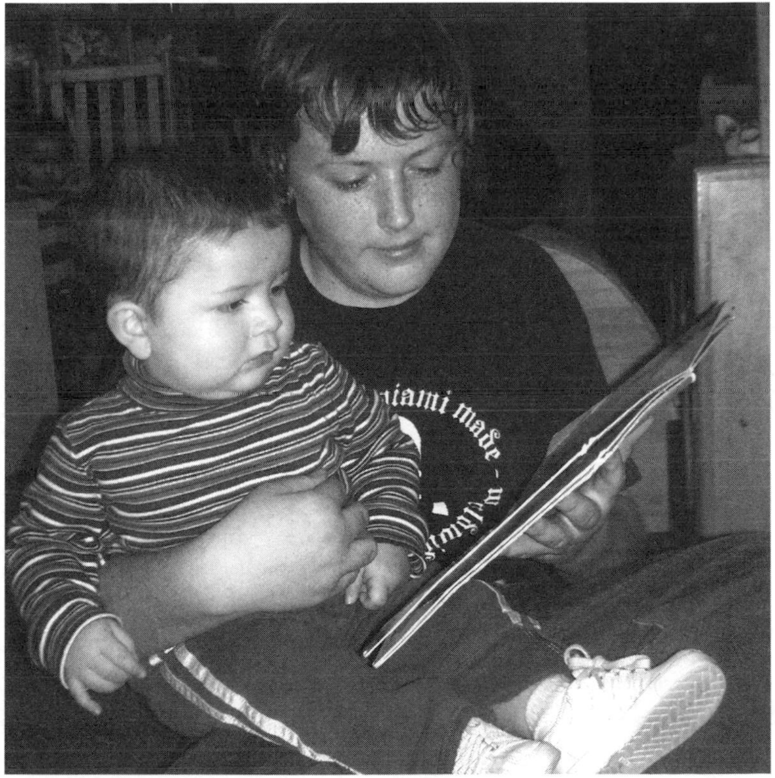

When he's reading with Dad, discipline is not a problem.

Toddlers and Discipline

Elena has always been a good baby, but she has her moments. Lately she's going through the Terrible Two stage where she wants to do only what she wants to do. Now she tells us "No." I try not to yell at her, and I don't want to hit her.

She'll go after something on the furniture, and we tell her not to get it. We tell her "No," and she looks at us, then takes it. We take it from her, and she'll take it again, then throw the stuff.

Carlos, 19 - Elena, 23 months (Monica, 18)

When this happens to you, don't yell. Get up and walk across the room. Tell your child what he should do as you move him away from what he can't have. If you yell your directions from a distance, he probably won't understand them. Even if he does, he's likely to ignore you. He has little understanding of "right" or "wrong," or what could happen as the result of his actions. He has no idea that the delicate vase he just grabbed could slip out of his hands and break until it has done just that.

Most toddlers are "good" if they happen to feel like doing what they should do and not doing what they should not. Support his desire for independence by getting rid of any limits you don't really need. Limits that are needed, such as staying out of the street, must be firmly and consistently maintained.

Being Yelled At Hurts Him

You know how parents yell and say you can't do this and you can't do that? I don't want to yell or hit my son because I don't think that teaches you anything. When I was little, l got hit. It didn't teach me nothing. If you get hit all the time, pretty soon it don't hurt no more. If he does real bad, I don't blow my top.

I think about it first, then talk about it with him, and tell him why he shouldn't do this. When he's a baby, there's no way he should be punished.

Jimmy, 17 - Roman, 1 year (Rosalva, 19)

No one should ever discipline a child in anger. Too often in anger, people use tactics they don't want their child to copy. They're rude. They yell, they use bad language, and they make horrible threats. Yelling is verbal abuse. It scares a child. It's hard on his self-esteem.

Poor self-esteem is a nasty stumbling block not only to good behavior, but to learning as well. If he feels he isn't a good person, he won't act like one. That's not what you want for your child.

We are our children's models. If we want our children to respect other people, we have to show respect for them. Yelling at him isn't showing respect.

Must Children Be Hit, Slapped, or Spanked?

Should children be slapped or spanked? Some people say, "Yes," but more and more people are saying "No." Usually they say "No" because they have discovered that spanking doesn't work very well.

I don't believe in hitting. I ain't going to hit my son. I was hit. I hate to see people hurt, in pain, and I don't want to see Jaysay cry. I don't want him to go through what I went through. I been in homes, I had a real bad coming up, but I don't want him to go through that.

Darrance, 17 - Jaysay, 1 year (Victoria, 17)

Hitting a child won't make her be obedient. There's no way you can force her to eat her dinner or to urinate in the toilet, for example. Spanking or slapping a child is not a good idea for many reasons. The baby or toddler will seldom understand why you, someone she trusts, hit her to make her cry. Even if she realizes that she displeased you, she now knows that hurting people is all right, especially if you're bigger and stronger. It must be — daddy or mother hit her. It's all right to be a bully!

Spanking does not teach them to stop. Hitting on them just makes them mad, and they do it again. But teaching — show them they're not supposed to mess with it. As they grow older, they'll know that's wrong.

When my family spanked me, I knew what I did was wrong — but it made me angrier and angrier, and I'd keep on doing it. I'd rob and everything, and they kept locking me up. Now that I have kids, I know there's no use treating them as I was treated.

Alton, 17 - Britney and Jakela, 1 year (Sharrell, 19)

Punishment Interferes with Learning

Punishment tries to control behavior by force, using pain and loss for effectiveness. It can interfere with learning because none of us learns as well when we're afraid. Punishment too often gives a child a feeling of failure.

You're closer to the one that doesn't spank you. I did what my dad said because he never hit me. Hitting isn't going to help anyway because you get hit and it's over. It don't make any difference.

Wayne, 17 - Ricky, 6 months (Charlene, 16)

Harsh punishment is emotionally scarring. While some children seek revenge, others become guilty and humiliated victims, people afraid to do anything for fear of failure. They don't learn to think for themselves.

Blind obedience is not the goal of discipline. Blind obedience will cause a child to be a follower who will do what other people tell her to do without judging whether it's right or wrong.

Child Abuse Happens

Another reason not to use hitting as punishment is the real danger of getting out of control. Physical child abuse is a tragic reality for many families in the United States. More than a million children are abused each year, and about 2,000 die from child abuse.

If a parent decides that hitting is a good method of punishment, that parent may be more likely to hit too hard than would the parent who doesn't believe in hitting in the first place. Parents who were spanked a lot or physically abused as children are more likely to abuse their children.

Males tend to be more aggressive, and around children you need to deal with this. Children don't need this. How do you deal with the frustrations and angers of parenting? Take time out. If you need a break, find someone else to hold your child for a little while. Let things simmer down a bit, and avoid thinking it's a power struggle.

It's not a power struggle with the child. He's just exploring his world, testing his boundaries, learning what he can get away with. He doesn't do this to anger or upset you.

Greg, 17 - Liana, 1 year (Nicole, 17)

Helping Your Toddler Behave

You can and should limit your toddler's behavior with necessary restrictions. You can and should stop his activities when necessary either by removing him from the scene or helping him do what he must do. It is part of your job as his parent.

Many parents resort to an occasional swat on a diapered bottom. Their child survives nicely, but the fact remains — that swat probably didn't accomplish much. A child who is spanked is actually less likely to obey in the future.

I change my tone of voice when she's naughty, but I don't spank her. I don't think that's right. I figure when you spank them, it just brings a fear against you. They fear you and then they hate you.

I got spanked, and I felt it would have been better if my father had sat down with me and talked with me and told me what I did wrong. That way I could understand, and I wouldn't do it again. When he hit me, I'd run outside and hide. It didn't bring any joy to me. I figure I'd love him more if he hadn't hit me.

Danny, 18 – Ashley, 15 months; Aaron, 3 weeks (Disiree, 16)

You can find discipline strategies that work without yelling, slapping, or hitting. Also take time to appreciate this delightful little person who is your child. Respect his need to explore and learn. Think about how you can help him succeed in his drive toward discovery. Then both you and your child will win.

Discipline Strategies

Strategy 1. Use "No" Sparingly.

"No" is an important word in discipline, but don't use it too often. Your goal when you say "No" is to get your child to react, to stop what she's doing. If she hears "No" every two minutes all day long, she's not going to respond.

We're just getting into discipline right now, and it's difficult. Liana's really getting a mind of her own. We try to use the word "No" as little as possible because otherwise it won't be effective.

We've taught her words like "hot," and she understands. We use distraction as much as possible. The "No" only works to an extent, and if you overdo it, you end up becoming frustrated.

Greg

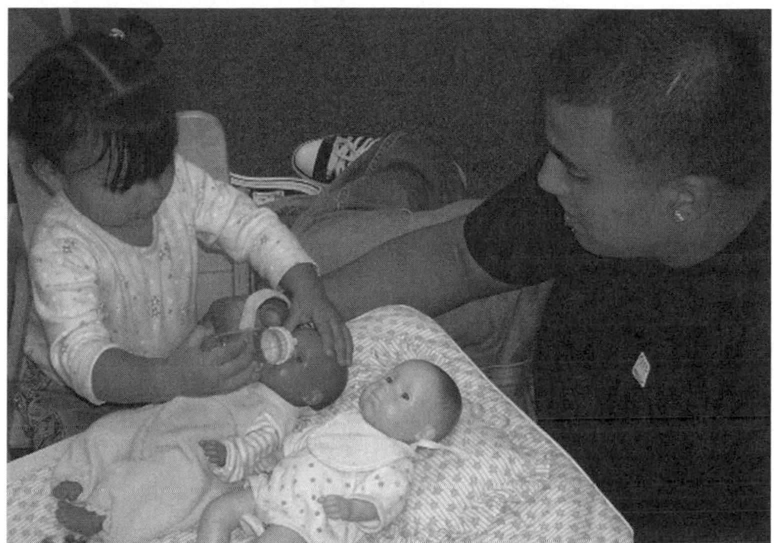

When you play with her, you won't need to say "No" very often.

If she hears "No" only a few times a day, and she hears a different I-mean-it tone of voice, she will learn to react and obey. That's what you want.

Strategy 2. Distract Her

When you distract her from an unwanted activity by giving her something else to play with, you can often do so without using the word "No" at all.

"Here's your ball. Can you roll it to me?" works much better than saying to a nine-month-old baby, "No, don't do that." This way, you're telling her what she should do.

Strategy 3. Positive Approach

It really bothers me when she says "No" and won't do what I tell her to do — especially when I know she knows exactly what I want. She won't look at me — she just sits there and won't do what I say.

John

Stoop down and get eye contact before you tell her what you want her to do. Then she'll be more likely to listen to you and understand what you're saying. She's getting a lot of information through your body language and facial expressions.

When you talk to her, give her positive rather than negative commands. Tell her what she should do rather than what she should not. Instead of saying, "Don't touch the vase," try "The vase needs to stay on the table." Instead of "Stop pulling the cat's tail," try "Let's pet the kitty gently."

Strategy 4. Communication and Respect

Discipline throughout childhood will be easier if you and your child can communicate easily. Talk to her as you change her diaper. At mealtime, tell her about the food she's eating.

As you talk to your child, you're telling her that all these things you do for her are more than just a duty you must perform. They are something you do because you truly care about her.

Communication with and respect for your child is important, whether she's a newborn, a toddler, or a teenager.

Strategy 5. Consistent and Balanced Life Style

Young children generally will eat better and get to sleep more easily if these events occur at about the same time every day. If your toddler is well-nourished and rested, he'll be a lot easier to manage.

He needs both active and quiet play. If he's too active, he may tire or get over-excited. Sitting quietly for very long is hard, too. His muscles need to move, and he must explore. A balance of active and quiet activities is best.

Strategy 6. Give Him a Choice

Give him a choice whenever you can. "It's time for your bath. Do you want it in the tub or in the shower?" may get his cooperation faster than ordering, "Take your bath now."

"Do you want lunch outside or in your high chair?" may make him more willing to leave his morning play than a command, "Come to lunch right now."

When you give him a choice, you're giving him a sense of control over his environment and a feeling of competence. This means he's less likely to defy you.

Keep the choices simple. Even then, he may have a difficult time sticking to his choice. For instance, if you ask him if he'd like apple juice or milk for his snack time, he may select the milk. Then he may become very upset if he can't have juice instead. Let him change his mind. That's all right.

Be sure the choices you give him are real. Don't ask him "Do you want to go to bed now?" if you've already decided he must go. Point to the clock and say, "It's time to go to bed now. Which bedtime story would you like me to read?"

Strategy 7. Reinforce Behaviors You Like

Reinforcing good behavior is an important part of discipline. If, when your child is playing quietly, you ignore him, his behavior is not being reinforced. Instead, join him in his play or talk about what he's doing. For instance, tell him, "I like the way you stacked those blocks." Or sit quietly and watch him play.

Mandi's thrown only a couple of tantrums so far. We give her a lot of praise when she's a good girl. That's a lot of the time, and we try to reinforce that.

We're fairly consistent. She really wants to be a good girl. I think a lot of that is attention. When you give them a lot of attention, they don't have to misbehave.

John

Toddlers need a lot of attention. Positive attention from significant persons makes learning more meaningful and important. Praise works so much better than punishment.

If she's getting your attention and companionship when she's behaving the way you want her to behave, she'll probably continue doing those things that draw the attention she craves. If she seems to get attention mostly through being naughty, she'll probably act naughty more often.

Strategy 8. Warning Before Activity Change

Many young children have a hard time changing activities. They become quite involved with what they're doing, and it's hard for them to stop.

Tell her a few minutes ahead of time when you want her to change her activity. Then she knows her play is about to be interrupted, and she can begin to think about what will happen next.

This will help her learn to anticipate and plan ahead. It will make the transition from one activity to the next much easier for both of you.

Strategy 9. Provide a Reward

A reward for a particular behavior should occur as a natural result of that behavior. For instance, tell her if she helps you pick up the toys, you'll have time to read her a story. If she cooperates in the supermarket, you'll stop at the park on the way home.

Many times the best reward is telling her that she did a good job and that you're proud of her. This is much more significant than saying she's a good girl. By recognizing her ability to do the task and to do it well, you help her feel competent. She'll feel able to learn even more.

Strategy 10. Time-Out May Help

Some people use time-out as a discipline technique. If the child is misbehaving, he is told to sit in a chair for a specified time. Usually a timer is used, and the parent says, "You may get down when the timer dings."

If you use time-out with a toddler, the time should be very short, perhaps a minute for each year of his age. Better yet, use time-out, but don't suggest that it's meant as a punishment.

When your toddler fusses, cries, or "acts out" and misbehaves, he's expressing distress. Hitting, biting, throwing toys or other objects may be an indication that the child has lost control of his behavior and may need help to regain it. Time-out might be that help.

Time-out need not be spent without any activity. It is not necessary or even desirable to set him on a chair in the corner. It can be time spent resting, or with a quiet activity away from noise and excitement or other stimulation. Your goal is not to punish your child, but to help and support him so he can get back in control.

Perhaps as he gets older, he will recognize his own need for rest and relaxation. This is more likely to happen if time-out has been a positive experience for him, and it has not been used to punish or embarrass him.

Strategies Instead of Punishment

You'll think of many other strategies that will work with your child. Using discipline strategies to help her behave appropriately makes childrearing much more effective than using punishment to force her to obey. With your discipline strategies, you not only help her learn self-control, you support her self-confidence. You give her self-respect.

Discipline begins with your relationship with your child. If you have a good relationship, he wants to please you just as you want to please him. You want to do things to make him feel good. He wants to do things to make you feel good.

Most important, good discipline demands an unending supply of love.

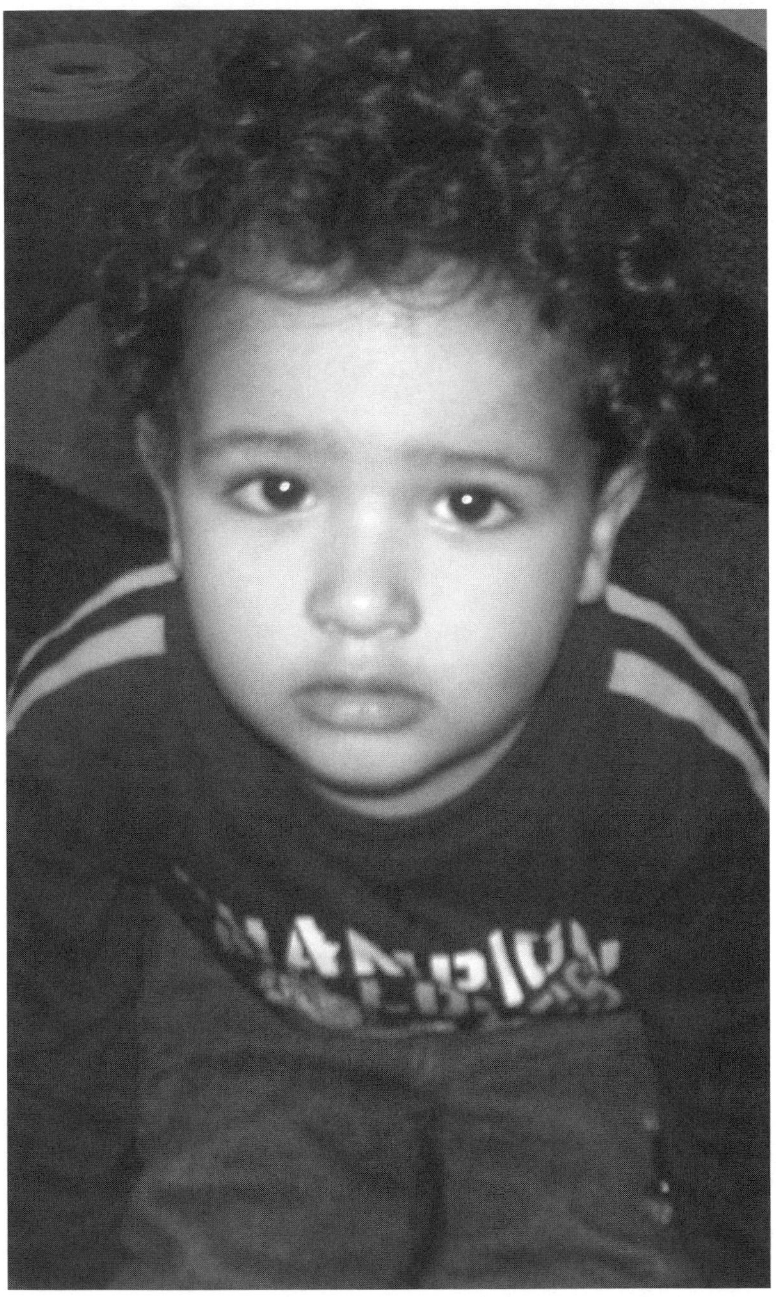

He wants to do everything you do.

12

Gang Involvement for Dads?

- **Why join a gang?**
- **Does gang involvement affect parenting?**
- **Gang clothes on babies?**
- **If you decide to leave**
- **Keeping guns and children separate**
- **Will your child join a gang?**
- **Teaching your child to be non-violent**
- **Dealing with angry feelings**

I'm more responsible now. I don't hang out with my friends and come home late. I was associated with a gang but that changed. I was jumped out.

A lot of my friends were in gangs and their lives changed too. When they have children they at least try to get out. They don't hang out with those people no more because it's not going to get you anywhere. I have a friend now who is in jail for life and he can't see his three kids. He talked to me about not being able to see his baby.

Marco, 18 - Lily, 1
(Serene, 18)

It was a choice between the gang and my daughter. The gang is too intense, and you need to be around them too much. The baby was a lot more important than being around my drinking buddies.

It was real hard to get out because I was pretty much one of the leaders. I let them alone now. I went to jail for awhile, and realized it wasn't worth it. I think it's more of a thing for younger kids actually. I think people stay in gangs because they get no respect elsewhere.

Zaid, 19 - Amber, 15 months (Tiffany, 20)

I've had guns pulled on me and that wasn't much fun. One time me and Lupe and my son were crossing the street, just walking home from the local park. A car cut us off as we were walking, and I was so upset I flipped the driver off. He decided to come back, himself and two women. He ended up pulling a gun on me. Lupe was pushing my son's stroller, and he was no older than 6 months.

Lupe broke into tears crying, "Don't shoot him," and I had nothing to say, it was such a shock. The girls in the car kept telling him to get back in the car, and he finally left.

I thought I'd keep my temper from here on. Someone else might react even more. I put my son's life in jeopardy. Before, when I was in a gang, I could take off running and not worry about leaving anybody behind. In this instance, I couldn't just leave.

Domingo, 22 - Lorenzo, 4 (Lupe, 21)

Why Join a Gang?

Thousands of young people across the country belong to gangs. They may join, be jumped in, before they reach their teens. They join a gang because they want to belong to something. They want to be part of a group. The support members give each other can be positive. They may feel protected from other gangs.

I was involved in a gang. Now that I have a daughter, it doesn't even cross my mind no more. I'm always going to talk to my friends, but whatever happened before . . . I'm trying to live a different life.

Just because you're in a gang doesn't mean you're a bad person, but you are more likly to go to jail and never see your kids again — or you might get killed. That's not what Brooke needs from her father.

Isaac, 18 - Brooke, 9 months (Alexis, 17)

Gang membership also may mean involvement with alcohol, drugs, stealing, involuntary sex, and violence. Gang violence is often reported in the newspapers, and gang members speak of seeing friends killed. Many schools are not safe for students because of gang activity.

Before, I would blow off and go down the street and look for somebody to beat up. That was me and I didn't care. But now I have my daughter, and I have to set an example for her.

I started in 7th and 8th grades, and when I got to my freshman year, I didn't care. I was all into it. But I still got good grades. I'd always do my homework, because I still had dreams. I didn't want to be at the same place doing the same things every day. I didn't want to be in jail, I didn't want to be strung out on drugs, on the corner asking for money. And then my brother, I always saw him incarcerated, in and out. I decided this had to stop now in our family.

Lucas, 21 - Kamie, 21 months (Kelsey, 19)

Does Gang Involvement Affect Parenting?

I used to be bad, I was on probation. I used to be in a gang, a long time ago. It started in sixth grade.

I got jumped in then. Basically, what a gang is, you have to show off in front of your friends what you can do. To me now it's stupid, it's not going to get me anywhere.

When I met Emilia, I gave my life to her, and she said I had to quit being a gang member. I quit. I still have friends, but a lot of my friends quit, too.

This is where life starts. You can't be bad the rest of your life. I got a job as soon as I found out Emilia was pregnant.

I'll try to find a better environment for Sancia. The whole world is bad, but there are some places where it's good. Right now I'm trying to do my best to raise her the best I can. I'm enjoying her.

Gavin, 17 – Sancia, 6 months (Emilia, 16)

If a gang member becomes pregnant, or is the father of a child, will involvement in the gang have any effect on their child? Is it possible to be a good parent at the same time he is actively involved with a gang? Riley doesn't think so:

I have been to meetings with gang members and they'd bring their kids. They'd be running around listening to what we said. We have all our guns, walking around, drinking, playing with the other kids, smoking weed, and the homeboys, the fathers, don't care. But at the time you don't really think about it because it's not your kids.

If I pounded somebody's face in, or I hit him with something, or he's in the hospital or I left him there to die, just because he's from a different neighborhood, I looked and thought, this is somebody's baby even if he is my age.

I looked at my son and thought, will he be like me? I thought, I might lose my son because of gang violence. My whole family is involved in the gang, my mother, my father, my uncles. I thought to myself, things have to change. Dorian is the next generation. He's the one who's going to school to learn, not be on the outside doing something wrong.

Now I can't just think of myself, I have my son to think of. I have a beautiful baby, and he needs a lot of love. When I don't have a job I feel so bad, and I come close to thinking of going out there and robbing, selling drugs, but things always come through. I like my new lifestyle now. I go to work, and I bring a pretty good sized paycheck home. Everything is going well right now, and we're getting married next year.

Riley, 18 - Dorian, 11 months (Karen, 17)

Sometimes within the gang a toddler is treated like a pet or a toy. Gang members may give little thought to his needs or even his safety. The love and nurturing the child needs may be hard to get.

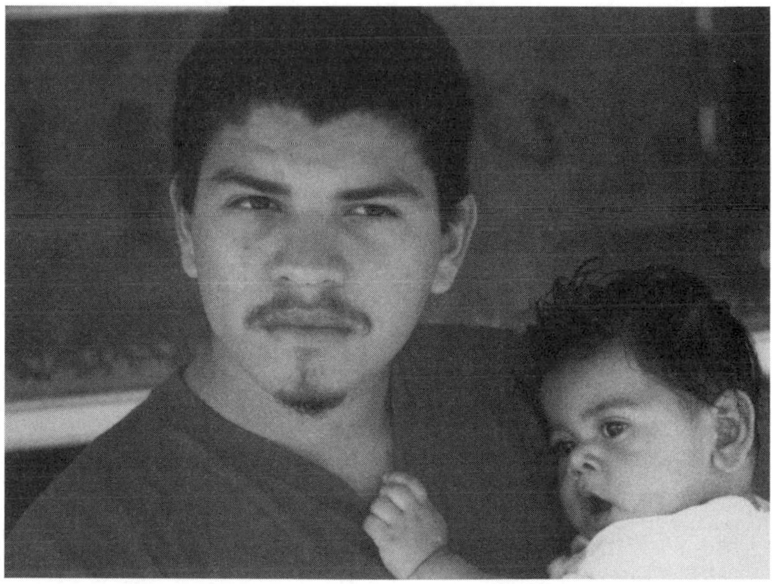

Now I have my son to think of.

Gang Clothes on Babies?

Babies and toddlers tend to be charming little people who generally look good no matter what they're wearing. Small children love to mimic their parents, and they usually think it's great if they're wearing clothes similar to mom's or dad's. Does this extend to gang attire? The young parents we interviewed don't think so.

I try not to dress my kids like gang people. I don't want them to be judged because of the way they're dressed. The way you dress kids is an indication of how you want them to grow up.

In our society clothes make a difference. I have noticed a lot of people, just because they're dressed in baggy clothes, they're thought of as gang members.

As you get older, common sense will tell you the gang is not getting you anywhere. Those kids are not going to put food on your table or a roof over your head.

Glen, 25 - Sergy, 3; Leonardo, 4 (Danica, 22)

If You Decide to Leave

Gangs vary a great deal, so it's hard to generalize. Many young people, however, decide parenthood is a reason to leave. When a gang member decides to leave, it's probably wise to assure members he is not rejecting them. He just can't handle the action or take the risks anymore. It's usually not necessary to reject them as people, as relatives, or even as friends.

It was pretty hard to get away from them. No gang lets you go just because you want to. But I was causing problems for them, and when my girl got pregnant, they were OK because that's how they got rid of me.

Mateo, 17 - Arcadia, 1 month (Rosalyn, 16)

Some gangs, however, make it extremely difficult for a member to get out. If you're in that situation, and you'd like to change your lifestyle, have you considered leaving your neighborhood? For some people, that appears to be the best solution. It's also likely to be an extremely difficult decision. Even if you'd like to leave, where would you go?

Is there a relative or close family friend who might take you in? Is an older sibling thinking of moving out, and might take you along? How about getting a roommate or other couple to move out of the area with you? Even a few miles away can make all the difference.

If you have no resources, and neither your parents, your relatives, your partner, or your friends can/will help you, you need to go elsewhere for help. Chief of Police Richard Tefank, Buena Park, California, commented, "Getting out takes trying to get some help. If you want to leave the neighborhood bad enough, I think you can.

"That can mean contacting local churches. At least you'd get some support there, and if you need to talk to somebody, it's a good place to go.

"Next, I'd try Child Protective Services. You go there and say, 'I want to get out of this environment with my child. Who could help me?' You aren't going as a Protective Services client. You're going there to seek help, and you might get a supportive social worker who might think, 'I'll help this person because if I don't, they may become my client.' If you don't have financial resources, no family support, it's going to be tough."

You might also find help by contacting some of the other helping resources listed in chapter 16.

Help *is* available, but you may have to work hard at finding the help you need to enable you to have the life you want for you and your child. *You and your child are worth the effort!*

Keeping Guns and Children Separate

Guns are one of the leading causes of death in children. Although many people have guns in their homes, seldom do they teach children how to handle them safely. Often they don't even keep the guns locked up in a safe place.

When young people handle guns, it can be dangerous not only to their enemies, but to family members and friends as well. It can also bring more violence to their home and family, increasing the chance that someone will be killed.

If you have a gun in your home, be sure it's locked away from your child. Don't put it in a glass case where he can see it. The gun should not be in sight, it should be unloaded, and the ammunition should be stored in a different place. You want to be absolutely sure your child or another child isn't killed by a gun in your home. An alarming number of guns in homes are used against family members.

Will Your Child Join a Gang?

If Avery joined a gang, I'd be outraged. I hope I can raise my son so he won't need to be in a gang. I want him to be strong enough that he'll be comfortable without that protection.

I think my anger management will help him not get angry — Kids follow what you do.

Todd, 18 - Avery, 6 months (Celia, 19)

Not one father or one mother I interviewed told me s/he wanted her/his son or daughter in a gang.

They talked about strategies which might prevent their child from going this route. They stressed the importance of staying involved with one's child, of "being there" for that child.

They talked about their parents who were too busy or too poor to support them in school or community activities, and of the difference being involved in sports, for example, might have made in their lives:

> *We want Dakota in sports. I believe the coach will teach the children the right way, teach them discipline, to be on time, to work hard. I noticed a difference when I was in sports and when I wasn't.*
>
> *When I was in sports, I got to meet a lot more people, and school became more interesting. You have to keep up your grades, and when I was keeping up my grades, I was learning more. When I wasn't in sports, I stayed home and watched TV. The road didn't seem to be going anywhere. I was just there.*
>
> Nathan, 20 - Dakota, 11 months (Zamdra. 18)

The relationship you build with your child is the most important factor in protecting him from gangs and violence.

Teaching Your Child to Be Non-Violent

Fighting gives more problems — you just have another enemy. If you talk something out, it will help you in the end. Maybe the enemy is not going to be a friend, but he'll have respect for you.

> *Gang life and being a father doesn't mix. You can't be a good father if your gang is there because your homies are going to want you to go out and party, and your child has to be fed. They don't go together.*
>
> Todd

You can't immunize your child against being the victim of a drive-by shooting, but you can help her learn ways of avoiding violence. Helping your child learn non-violent techniques for settling disagreements is a gift you can give her that can last a lifetime.

It starts with the relationship you build with your child. The bonding that happens between a father and his newborn, a mother and her newborn, is where it begins. The result of that bonding is healthy attachment between you and your child. This attachment is extremely important for your child's development. Language skills are basic. If you keep your relationship strong, it should be fairly easy to talk together, and that provides some protection for your child. It helps him learn to use words rather than violence.

A child learns to be violent when her parents are violent. When dad and mom fight, yell, and hit each other, or hit her if she misbehaves, she'll see fighting and hitting as ways to solve problems. It must be all right to hit people. The persons who mean the most to her hit.

If you model nonviolence in your daily life, in your actions with your child as well as with other people, he is likely to follow your example.

Dealing with Angry Feelings

Even if you've grown up with violence around you, you can learn better techniques for handling problems. It's important to learn these techniques, not only for you, but even more for your child's sake. You can help your child learn ways of dealing with angry feelings in nonviolent ways.

There was a time when many people expected their sons to fight. A boy who refused to fight was labeled a sissy. Some people still feel this way. This kind of thinking was based on the assumption that boys were not likely to be seriously injured in a fist fight. Guns were not supposed to be part of the deal. Now, however, the widespread use of guns drastically changes the situation.

> *I'll teach my son that if he can walk away from the problem, walk away. But if the problem is going to follow you, you may have to handle it. But you have to think it through. What's going to happen if I beat up this guy and he gets a gun?*
>
> Riley

Being able to walk away is important, and sometimes it's a really hard thing to do. Your feelings are hurt, you're angry. Some people are too afraid to simply walk away.

Counting to ten before reacting helps some people calm down. Sometimes cracking a joke will cut the tension. Walking away from an argument may be the best approach. Then angry feelings have a chance to cool down. Usually, expressions of anger only create more problems.

Your child watches your response in any dispute. From his observations, he gets ideas on how to respond. He's likely to copy the strategies he thinks work. When you avoid conflict, you're helping your child. From your example, he's learning safer ways to handle situations that could become dangerous.

> *What I learned from the streets myself, you can either turn the other cheek or you can stand up and fight, but to stand up and fight may not be the right thing to do. I want him to understand there are consequences to every act he takes. I hope he can speak his way out of it.*
>
> Domingo

Encourage your child to talk to you. Really listen to him as he tries to express his thoughts and feelings. This will help him gain confidence in his ability to use words. With your help, his use of language will continue to grow and improve. He will become more able to talk to other people and solve problems with words. You are helping your child learn how to use words instead of fists or guns.

This skill could save your child's life.

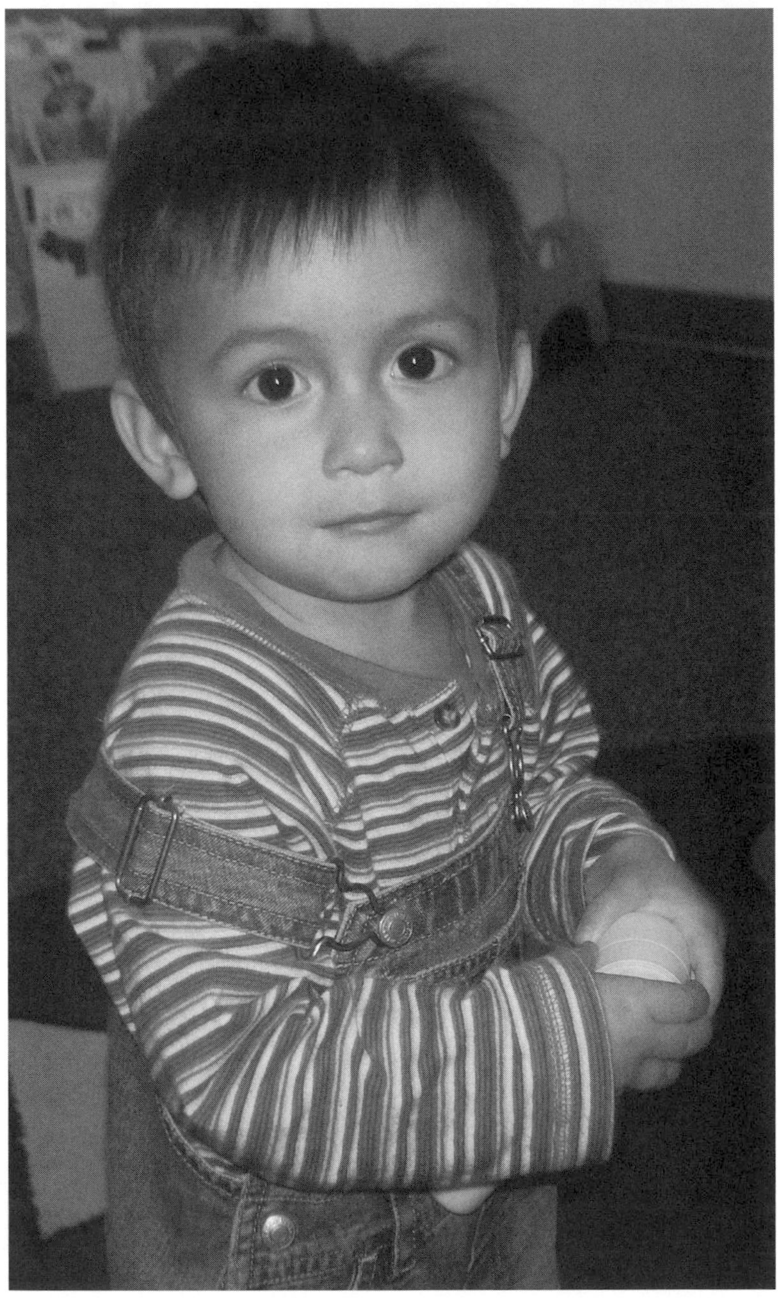

Communicating with him while you're away is important.

13

Staying in Touch When You're Away

- **If you must be away**
- **Keeping in touch through letters**
- **Going beyond letter-writing**
- **If your child isn't born yet**
- **Can they visit you?**
- **More tips for incarcerated fathers**
- **Going home may be difficult**
- **Your child needs you**

I was there with her for the first six months. But then I got in trouble with the law and they put me away for six months, actually five months for good behavior.

I was really disappointed with myself. It's the worst feeling you can get to be in there and wondering how she's doing, while you're there wasting your time and doing nothing when you could be out here working and supporting her. Lots of stress knowing you have to go to court to see what they will do with you.

I didn't see her or my

daughter, only once did I see Natalia. I didn't get to see my child be born. I couldn't go to the birth.

Geraldo, 17 - La'Keshia, 2 months (Natalia, 15)

If You Must Be Away

Some couples who are "together" are separated for months or even years. He or she may be in jail. He or she may be in the armed forces. Or there could be other reasons for their separation. If you're an absent parent, you know how much effort and determination it takes to remain close to your partner and your child.

Do you know much about child development? Where is your child at this point? What is your child doing right now? What is going on with him?

If you must be away, try to stay focused on that development and on the characteristics of your child. You'll be more likely to maintain a relationship with her. Does she like or hate broccoli? Does she enjoy taking a bath? These are things you can talk/write about with/to your child.

If a parenting class is available, taking it might help you understand better the stages through which your child is going. You'd have an idea of the behavior to expect when you return home.

Do the best you can to keep track of what's going on. Even though you're away, stay in with your child as much as you can. Get information about how he's doing developmentally, changes in his attitude.

How does he act around this person, then around someone else? Keep learning as much as you can. Even though you're away, you can still know how fast he's growing, how he's progressing, the funny things he does. Mostly, I use the telephone, and write about two letters a week. Melinda tells me a lot about Kory, and she sends some photos.

Marc, 16 - Kory, 14 months (Melinda, 18)

Encourage his mother to send you photos of your child and to describe his activities to you. The more aware you are of your child's development and of his activities, the more possible it will be to renew your relationship with him when you can be together again.

I sent letters to her, and she would tell me how she was doing, how the baby was getting bigger. I was sometimes crying because there was that one day when they let her come in. I got to see her Jan. 6 and the baby was born a day later. She sent me pictures of her belly getting bigger. She sent me an ultrasound. When I got the ultrasound, it was 3-D and you could see his face real clear. I put it on my wall and I'd look at it every day, and I'm saying, I'm going to do good today so I can see you tomorrow.

He was almost a month old when I got out. We are living together, with my parents. It's keeping me out of trouble because I have to go home to my son and my girlfriend and help them. Now it's not only about me, it's about my son.

Geraldo

Incidentally, be assured that whether your child is a boy or a girl, s/he needs you. Your daughter needs a father as much as your son does.

Keeping in Touch Through Letters

Barry McIntosh is a parent educator in the New Mexico Young Fathers Project, Santa Fe, New Mexico. He leads a Thursday night support group of incarcerated young fathers each week. A big question, he points out, is how to stay in touch with one's child and the child's mother when Dad's away. He stresses the importance of writing to the child as well as the mother.

"They say, 'But my kid can't read yet,'" McIntosh commented, "but I remind them that at 10 years of age, their child *can* read that letter. I ask if they think that would be a letter they'd keep if their dad wrote it, perhaps even before they were born. And they all reply, 'Yes!'"

Toddlers love to get mail. If you aren't with him, write to him a lot. Write short letters. Tell him. "Daddy loves you and wants to hold you in his arms." Identify yourself as "Daddy" at least three times in each letter so that he hears that special word. Write often.

> *I write to my son, a one-page letter, how I think about him, how much I love him. They told me I should just write it to show him I care about him and that I'm thinking about it. So I do it every two weeks.*
>
> Todd, 18 - Avery, 6 months (Celia, 19)

Remember that whoever takes care of him and reads your letters to him usually calls you by your first name or nickname. You can help your child know you as "Daddy" through these "daddy" letters.

Send your picture to him, date it, and sign it, "With love to (child's name), Daddy." It can be put on the refrigerator where he'll see it often.

Going Beyond Letter-writing

If you're artistic, illustrate your letters. Or compose a rap song for your child.

If it's possible to telephone him, do so. Even if he can't talk yet, he'll hear your voice and associate it with the word "daddy" and your picture.

When you're away from your child, for whatever reason, taping your voice, perhaps talking to him as well as reading a story, is a good way to remind him of you and of how much you love him.

Of course it was disappointing to leave them. I probably won't be in my son's life for about two years. I'm in the young fathers' project here (Juvenile Detention Center).

They tape-record me once a week reading a child's book. I don't get my visits because they moved across the country three months ago, but Avery hears my voice each week on those tapes. Celia says she plays the tape each night before he goes to sleep.

Todd

If you're incarcerated, you already know how important it is to stay out of trouble in the detention center so you can get phone calls and visits.

If Your Child Isn't Born Yet

I was 16 when my girlfriend got pregnant. At the time I was in jail, I had gotten into a lot of trouble. I found out when she was already two or three months pregnant.

We couldn't talk because in the juvenile system she couldn't visit me. I was in jail for eight months and we talked five times during that time. My mom kept in touch and told me how Chanda was doing.

Kobe, 19 - Maricio, 14 months (Chanda, 16)

If your partner is pregnant, she may complain that you aren't involved in her pregnancy. Writing to her — and to your unborn child — concerning your excitement about your child or your scary feelings about being a father may help.

I haven't seen Sophia since she found out she's pregnant, although we thought she probably was. She writes me letters, tells me her stomach is getting big, and the baby is kicking a lot. But what can I do?

Alvaro, 17 (Sophia, 6 months pregnant)

Perhaps she'll send you pictures of her as the baby develops. Tell her how much you'd like a copy of the ultrasound showing your baby. Ask her to tell you about her visits with her healthcare provider. How is she feeling? Your interest can make her feel better.

Can They Visit You?

I think I'm going to get out pretty soon. My P.O. wants me out. He knows I have two kids, and I was working and going to an alternative school. I'm in the fathers' group here.

I was yelling and cussing at my kids, but I've learned a lot in the parenting group here.

As soon as we're in the parenting class, we get to see our kids on Sundays, 9-10. There are toys out there and we get to visit with our kids.

The first time Kolleen came here to see me, she started crying, and I started crying. She got scared and didn't want to come to me. She got used to it. I found that when I stopped crying, she would come to me.

Leanne and I keep our relationship going through letters, the phone, my mom. We're still together. It's really hard and complicated, different than when we were living together.

Santos, 17 - Kolleen, 17 months; Jameka, 5 months (Leanne, 16)

An incarcerated father may wonder how to react to visits from his child's mother. McIntosh suggests, "First, understand her. She has a right to be pissed off. You abandoned her and left her to raise this kid by herself. You have to understand, and you have to actively listen. Once she feels understood, she's less likely to complain and nag. Also understand that she is the single parent right now and she is calling the shots.

"Say 'May I hold the baby?' rather than 'Give me my baby.' When the child does come in, do as much attachment and bonding with that child as possible. If he's a newborn, hold him and look in his eyes. Also take cues from the baby – if he insists on staying with Mom, that's okay.

"Some of the guys don't want their child to see them incarcerated, perhaps because they had experienced this with their father. We talk about how the child will feel – does he really know where you are? It may be hard for you, but what are the needs of your child? A lot of the guys step up to fatherhood really well," McIntosh explained.

More Tips for Incarcerated Fathers

Mara Duncan is a teacher working with incarcerated men at the West Detention Facility, Richmond, California. She reports that some fathers feel they have no right to communicate with their child. They're ashamed, and wonder if it might be best not to let their child know where they are. Duncan suggests that they look at it from the child's perspective. It's usually best to be honest with the child rather than abandoning him.

"Fathers who are separated from their children need to find allies," Duncan said. "I suggest, 'Talk to the grandmother, the aunt, and show them you want to be part of your child's life.'

"First time, the father might hold his child and kiss him once. Next time, he'll hold him and kiss him twice. Next time, maybe he can stay 15 minutes. When the mother and other relatives see he's sincere, they may come around."

If a father is in jail and can't make his child support payments, he should get a letter written to the judge asking if payments can be stopped until he gets out. He might find it extremely difficult to make back payments when he gets out of jail.

Going Home May Be Difficult

> *Back when we were together, I was around all the time. I was still going places with my friends, but if Shawnté needed me, I wouldn't go out. I was with the baby a lot.*
>
> *Then I started getting in more trouble in the streets. I was always getting locked up, and finally I was sent away. Shawnté was sending me pictures, then all of a sudden I came home, and it was a whole lot different.*
>
> *I came over to see the baby, and we sort of stared at each other. I don't know what happened. I got out and everything changed. A lot of arguments came between us. We stopped talking to each other, and she don't want me around the baby.*
>
> *I tried to talk to her, but every time I talk, she have an attitude. Then I get angry, and I say I'm through with it. Then I think about my baby, and I talk to her again, but she don't want to see me.*
>
> *I think I should help take care of the baby even though we're apart. It's both our responsibilities.*
>
> *Even if Shawnté doesn't want to be with me, that's still my responsibility. We don't have to talk. I made that child. He's part of me.*
>
> Jamal, 16 - Valizette,16 months (Shawnté)

If Shawnté won't let him see his child, Jamal needs to talk to a lawyer to learn about his rights, as discussed in Chapter 16. In most states, unless the court rules otherwise, the father has a right to see his child. It's better, of course, to be with your child simply because you and the child's mother agree this is best for your child.

Jamal's best chance of having a satisfying relationship with Valizette might be to talk out his differences with Shawnté. They don't need to have a close relationship even if they are both going to parent this child. However, they need to be willing to talk to each other and to be civil to each other for their child's sake.

Your Child Needs You

I hope I get a letter from Teresa today. I think we're staying close. Any time I get to make a phone call, which is once a week, I call her. I write to her almost every day. If she doesn't write me, I keep writing her anyway.

Casey, 15 (Teresa, 6 months pregnant)

If you're away for awhile, know that your child needs you. Keeping in touch with him, and, if possible, with his mother, may help all of you to adjust better when you return home.

Usually, your life and your child's life will be better because you are maintaining a relationship with each other.

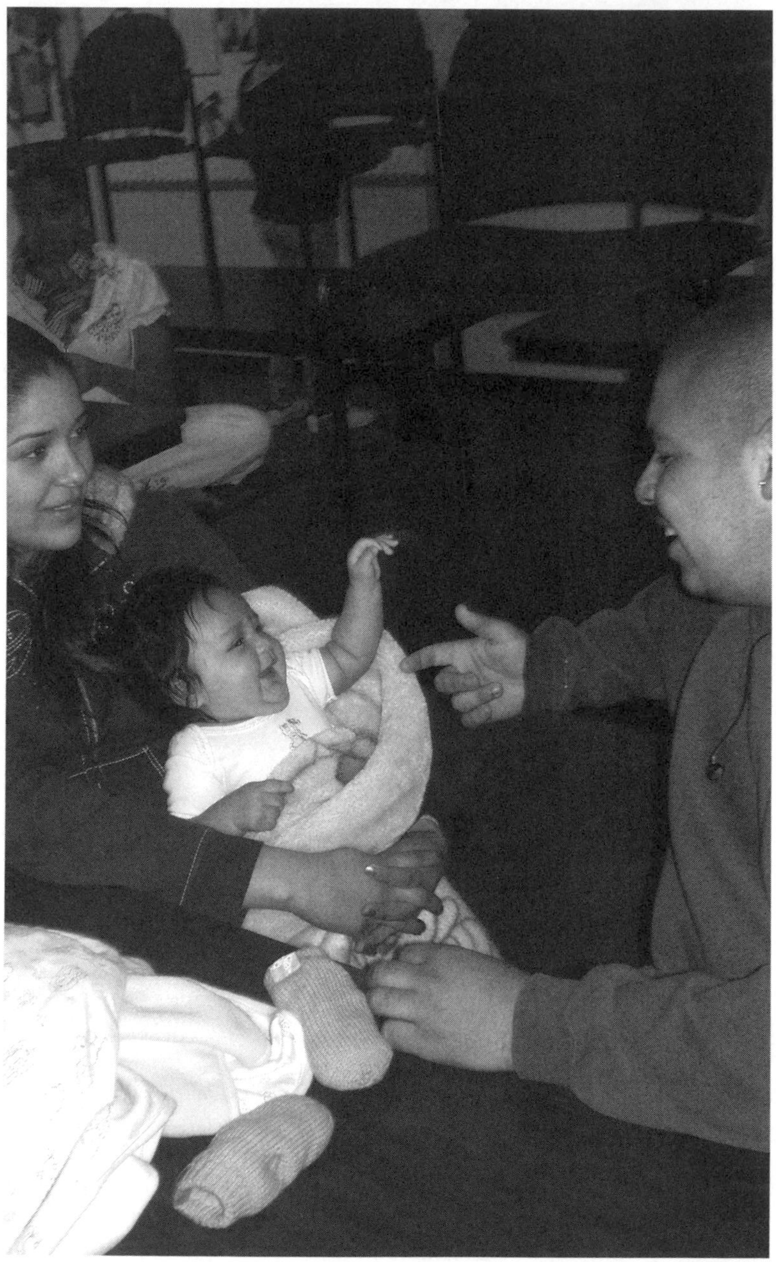

Maintaining a good relationship with your partner is important to your child.

14

Your Partnership — Another Challenge

- **Is marriage the answer?**
- **Making the marriage decision**
- **Does money matter?**
- **Stresses of living together**
- **Three-generation living**
- **People are not for hitting**
- **When parents separate**

I remember those first months it was really tough. A lot of times my parents had to give us money just to buy food. We were barely making it. My sister lives with us to help with expenses.

My girlfriend and my sister didn't always get along either. Somebody didn't wash their own dishes, it was bad, always something.

Javier, 28 - Salim, 9; Khalid, 6 (Shenca, 26)

Lynette thinks I don't really pay attention to her any more, that I give all my attention to the baby, but it's not really like that. What I'm doing is that you go for the little one now because she's something new. She looks at me with that face full of life, and I want to play with her. Lynette thinks I'm pushing her away.

Jacob, 19 - Sophie, 7 months (Lynette, 18)

Parenting is a difficult thing. It takes its toll on both parents. Mothers need to understand that it's very difficult for fathers, and the fathers need to understand that the mothers need a break.

At least once a month they need to go out separately with their friends. You also need to make time throughout the month for you two to do something together. You need time to nurture and build a relationship.

Greg - 17 - Liana, 1 year (Nicole, 17)

In some ways our relationship has improved, but other ways, it's more stressful.

Being unmarried, Jennifer sometimes has doubts about whether I want to be tied down to her and Katie. But other times it's better because we have a baby.

Ryan, 17 - Katie, 7 weeks (Jennifer, 18)

The relationship between a teen father and his child's mother may range from marriage to no relationship at all. How you parent your child depends somewhat on your relationship with his mother. You can be a "good" parent whether or not you and his mother are friends, but it's harder if you're not.

Less than one in five teenage mothers is married when her child is born. By the time the child is 3, a high percentage of these marriages have ended. By this time, many teenage parents are with different partners.

Making good decisions concerning partners is perhaps one of the hardest issues faced by teenage parents. There is likely to be even more heartbreak in a failed relationship when there is a child involved.

Is Marriage the Answer?

Marriage? I don't think any time soon, although I really want to because I love Alexis. I want my daughter to grow up with both of us, and I don't mean like with me just going to visit her once in awhile.

We just don't feel we're ready for marriage until we're a little older.

Isaac, 18 - Brooke, 9 months (Alexis, 17)

Are you thinking about marriage? Or maybe you're already married.

Thirty years ago, marriage was often the "answer" to too-early pregnancy. A pregnant teen's father might demand that his daughter and her boyfriend get married.

Some couples had many years of happiness together. For many other couples, it didn't work. Teenagers change rapidly as they grow older.

A boy and girl who marry at 16 may no longer share the same interests at 20. They may be two very different people. A couple married at 16 is much more likely to separate than is the couple who marries after 22.

If there is something wrong with the relationship now, marriage won't fix it.

Making the Marriage Decision

If you and your partner are considering marriage, you may want to discuss such things as:

- Do you have a place to live? For most couples, it's harder to develop a good relationship while you're living with other people.
- Do you both want to spend all the rest of your life together?

- Are you working and earning enough to support your family? Or will you and your partner both work and share in the care of your child?
- Do you agree on such important questions as:
  - When will you have your next child?
  - Will either or both of you continue going to school?
  - Who is expected to have a job? Husband? Wife? Both?
  - Who will take primary responsibility for the care of your child?

You can think of a lot of other things you need to discuss thoroughly before you decide to spend the rest of your lives together.

Does Money Matter?

Money, of course, cannot buy happiness, but the lack of it can cause problems. Javier thinks getting a raise at work probably saved his relationship with Shenca:

One day when the baby was six months old, Shenca was crying. I asked what was wrong, and she said this isn't what she expected. "This is just not what I wanted, or how I want to live," she said. I told her that this is all I can do for you. I told her this was all we had for now, but we would try to make it better.

She said, "It's not you. I just didn't imagine it like this. The baby never stops crying."

We talked for a while, 3-4 hours, and after that she didn't tell me again she didn't want this. Maybe because, as the months passed by, I started moving up in my job, I got a raise and a promotion. I think if I had made less money, I don't think we would have made it. When we didn't have enough money to go out, we couldn't relax. Even if it was just going to

McDonald's it helped, but those first six months we didn't because we didn't have any money. We ate sandwiches and canned food because Shenca didn't know how to cook and I didn't either. We ate at my mom's house quite a bit, and she cooked for us.

We're still together. About four years later we got married after our second child was born. I think it worked out pretty good for us.

Javier

If you live with her parents or yours, are you able to help with expenses? Tim moved in with Jocelyn's family with the agreement that he could live there until he finished school.

In the beginning it was real good. Now her mom is asking for money from me. The whole agreement was that I was only supposed to stay there until I finished school. But we had the baby and I can't be without my daughter so her mom let me stay there.

I'm beginning to look for my own apartment, whether with my girlfriend or not. It's a big thing. But I stay calm and deal with it. Starting now I have to pay $100/week. Do you think that's fair?

Tim, 20 - Chamique, 21 months (Jocelyn, 19)

Tim is working, and Jocelyn's mother has a right to ask him to pay rent if he continues to live there. If he and Jocelyn continue their relationship, they need to discuss their alternatives. Perhaps they'll decide to move out together.

Stresses of Living Together

Erica thought about abortion, but decided to continue the pregnancy. A week or two later we decided to get married. She moved in here with me and my parents until Kevin was born. Living with each other

She likes being with both Dad and Mom.

is tough. When we were that young we really didn't know each other as good as we thought — it was almost our first relationship.

It's hard living with your parents, too. I'd have to say, "Don't start with the marriage right away. You don't need to get married."

We lived here the whole time. We went through Lamaze. The pregnancy was hard. I finally got a job, and I worked after school every day plus weekends and holidays.

I was very tired all the time. Erica thought when we got married we'd spend more time together. Because of me working, we actually had less time. She'd say, because she was young, "Don't go to work today," but I had to.

When I'd come home, she'd want to play. I'd say, "I'm really tired right now," and she thought I was rejecting her.

Zach, 19 - Kevin, 20 months (Erica, 16)

If you're living together, your relationship will have its ups and downs, just as an older couple would experience. You may have added stress because of lack of money and dependence on your families. One or both of you may still be in school. Juggling school, parenting, and possibly a job can get crazy. Having a good relationship in the middle of all this stress is difficult.

Good relationships take time and effort in addition to love, just as good parenting takes time and effort in addition to love. Finding time for both your partner and your child may seem almost impossible.

Friday night we go to the movies. I feel it's very important that a couple spend time with each other. You need the time away, and it helps keep your relationship going. Having a child is such a responsibility, it gets to be overwhelming at times.

Dennis, 17 - Alexis, 6 months (Tara, 20)

Making time for each other may be difficult, but it's important to your relationship. Sometimes people talk about a good relationship being a 50-50 situation — each partner has equal rights and responsibilities. A better percentage is probably 60-60 — each partner goes more than half way to please the other.

At the same time, each of you needs to guard his/her own self-esteem. You do this even as you do more than your share in maintaining a loving and caring relationship.

Being honest and trusting with each other is essential.

Three-Generation Living

If you and your partner live with your parents or hers, this may add stress to your relationship.

Her parents are a lot different than mine. Her mom always had to add her two cents in on everything we did. She was practically telling us how to raise Deziree. It was rough.

We tried to make it work. We stayed out of the house as much as possible. We'd take Deziree to the park or to a friend's house.

Generally we just took it. We figured they're giving us this place to stay, and we have to take it until we can get our own place. We've lived here for a year.

Now we finally have enough money to move into our own apartment.

Parnell, 18 - Deziree, 18 months (April, 20)

Being somebody's son and following the rules of the house can be frustrating when you're also someone's dad, and you've taken on adult responsibilities. You'll feel less stress if you accept your current situation and make it work as well as possible — while you work hard toward becoming self-sufficient and able to support your family.

When I moved in it was pretty much all right. The only thing I didn't like was I was used to eating different stuff. And I was always outside playing around with my friends, and now that I moved down here I don't know no one. Sometimes I get frustrated or bored.

My relationship with Lynette's parents is pretty much okay. We live in the fixed-up basement and I don't really go upstairs except to eat.

Jacob

People Are Not for Hitting

With Celia it was pretty difficult. We'd fight, and I hit her a couple of times. She put me in check and said, "You don't do this. Either I'm leaving you or you're getting help."

So we went to counseling. I don't know why I did

that except that's what I was used to seeing. When I hit her I felt all bad, like less than a man. I'd get this feeling all through my body that I can't believe I did that. Celia helped me, and I don't do that any more.

Todd, 19 - Avery, 6 months (Celia, 19)

Some teenage (and older) men resort to hitting their partner when they're frustrated. Sometimes the woman beats on the man, but it's the woman who is most likely to be hurt. And no one wins an argument by using force or physical strength.

If you resort to violence, she won't agree with you because you're right, but because you're physically stronger. Beating someone doesn't solve problems, and it doesn't help a relationship. It makes things worse.

A man who hits a woman, he must not really be a man. There are ways to handle a situation without physical contact. That's wrong. I never hit my lady friend. We get into arguments, but when I get angry, I walk away. It doesn't take violence.

Jamal, 16 - Valizette, 16 months (Shawnté, 17)

Learn to argue without hitting each other. There are better ways to solve problems than hitting:

When I get frustrated, I leave. I go running, do something like that. That way I don't take it out on my girlfriend or my kid.

Tony, 16 - Felipe, 16 months (Alicia, 17)

There has been some hitting — that's why I got locked up in jail. It happened three years ago, and we started with a little jealousy. We'd get into arguments, and she'd start scratching me in the face, and I ended up pushing her. I ended up going to jail for that. I turned myself in for that warrant.

Ever since that day, me and her never fought again. The day I came back, I went to see her and I said, "Let's go for a walk." We're talking, and I told her I'm sorry for what I did and I'll never do it again. She told me she loved me and didn't want anything to happen to our relationship.

We worked the jealousy thing out. We figure that if the jealousy keeps up we'll end up hating each other.

Danny, 18 – Ashley, 15 months; Aaron, 3 weeks (Disiree, 16)

If you know someone who is being abused, you might want to suggest ***Breaking Free from Partner Abuse*** by Mary Marecek (1999: Morning Glory Press). This book offers help for women in abusive relationships. It's underlying theme is, "You don't deserve this."

When Parents Separate

The relationship with your partner may be more complicated because you're a parent. If it's a poor relationship, you may, because of your child, not feel free to leave. If you do split, however, you can continue parenting your child.

Our relationship is not going to work. There are too many bad parts about it.

That crushes my heart, not having the kids. I'm used to putting them to bed, kissing them in the morning before I go to work. I'll still get to see them.

I know the kids are going to ask why I left mom. I hope she'll explain why. I'd never say anything bad about their mother. When my mom and dad divorced, they talked bad about each other, and I didn't know what to think. I was confused. Sometimes I'm scared that my children won't really know me because they won't see me every day, only on weekends.

Luis, 20 - Benito, 8 months; Karina, 3 (Myndee, 21)

When the mother and father split up, the mother is more likely to have the day-to-day responsibility of child rearing. When this happens, dad needs to make an effort regularly to spend as much time as possible with his child. Some fathers get custody when the couple splits. Zach and Erica were married a year, then divorced. Zach continues to live with his parents and care for his child. Erica visits Kevin regularly:

> *We'd get in fights, and Erica would leave. She'd take a walk or go over to her mom's. I'd get all scared and go look for her.*
>
> *Finally Erica and Kevin moved back to her mom. They wanted me to pay a baby-sitter so she could start school, but I wasn't making enough money. Then one night I was at a friend's, and I guess Erica was all fed up. She brought Kevin over here and left.*
>
> *The next day I told her we'd keep Kevin. She said I'd never let her see him, and I said she could see him whenever she wanted. Kevin has stayed here since then. We've been divorced for several months. Mom helps me, but I've taken most of the responsibility.*
>
> Zach

Would you like to have custody of your child? If you aren't with your baby's mom, and you're concerned that she is not being responsible, talk with someone about the possibility of getting custody. Perhaps your mom, an aunt, or other responsible adult could help you consider your options.

There are no easy answers, but your concern for your child will help you work through your realities. Do the best you can wherever you are in your relationship with your child's mother. And remember — *your child needs you.*

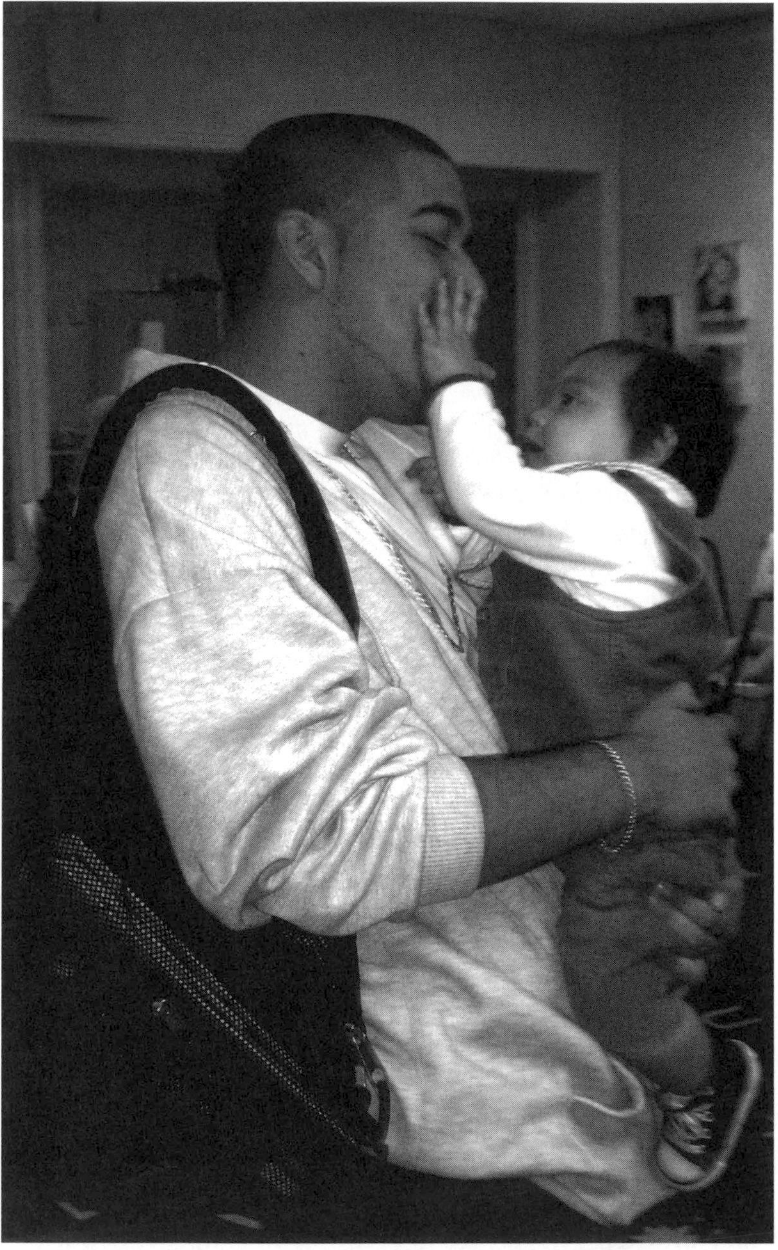

Some couples choose to delay their next pregnancy so they can give this child the care he needs.

15

Another Baby? But When?

- **Planning your family**
- **Lots of options**
- **Teen fathers comment on condoms**
- **Birth control injections**
- **Birth control pill**
- **Contraceptive patch, implant, IUD**
- **Emergency contraception**
- **STI concerns**
- **AIDS — incurable STI**
- **Caring for yourself and your family**
- **Planning for your next child**

Another baby? Not very soon. We're pretty careful with contraception because we don't want another baby right away. That would be hard because we'd be spending twice as much on diapers and everything else. It would make everything harder.

It'll also be easier when Keegan is 3 or 4 years old because he'll know more. He won't cry as much. We've agreed to wait.

Randy, 17 - Keegan, 2 months
(Whitney, 15)

A lot of people have too many babies and can't support

them. I want to be able to give Shaquille what he needs. Both Traci and I have a responsibility for birth control. I'm using a condom and she's on the pill.

Lester, 17 – Shaquille, 16 months (Traci, 16)

Planning Your Family

Many teen mothers and fathers who have one child are able to continue their education and work toward their goals. If they have a second child before they finish school, the difficulties multiply. Having more than one child limits one's independence drastically.

Many teen couples get pregnant again. Half of all teen mothers have another baby within two years. This happened to Santos and Leanne, and Santos advises:

Think about it before you have a second baby. It's not that wonderful. If you don't have a stable home for them, it's real crazy.

It's hard on my kids right now, and I'm really young and it's hard on me. For even the first one, wait until you have the stable home.

Santos, 17 – Kolleen, 17 months; Jameka, 5 months (Leanne, 16)

Couples need to think and talk about future family plans. How soon do you want another child? Many young mothers and fathers, whether married or not, don't want another baby right away. There are many reasons for waiting:

- You want to give your first child the care he needs. Toddlers need a great deal of attention.
- Outside care for one child is hard to find. Finding someone to care for two children is even harder.
- More babies cost more money. Do you have enough?

Financially difficult? Oh yes. It's like you're never through needing stuff. Chanté is always needing things and everything costs. ***Always.*** *Every time*

I look up, it's "Get me some more clothes or some more diapers."

Tiger, 19 – Chanté, 18 months (Crystal, 18)

- She's less likely to have a healthy baby if her next pregnancy happens too soon after the first one.
- Having too many children could hurt your relationship with your partner.

Babies do come by accident. If you don't want another child right away, birth control is essential. This could be simply not having intercourse, but most parents will want some other kind of contraceptive. If she's breastfeeding, don't count on it to keep her from getting pregnant. She can get pregnant even though she's breastfeeding.

We're really into it. I don't take the pill, but we always use the condom and foam. Neither of us will do anything if we don't have protection. Either one of us will say, "Do you have a condom? Foam?"

Erin, 16 - Alex, 12 months (Brian, 20)

Sexually active couples need to discuss their thinking concerning contraception. If this is difficult for you, remember that having another baby too soon would also be hard on your partner. Brad talked about this issue:

I'd rather have three years between children. I want my first son to have time for me to teach him.

How to talk about sex with your partner? First of all, be alone. Ask her how she feels about using protection. How many kids do you want to have? If one or the other doesn't want to use protection, they have to talk it through.

Brad, 17 - Maria, 13 months (Carole, 16)

Some young women say their partners don't want them to use birth control. One student told me her boyfriend wouldn't "let" her use birth control. He thought if she did, she might have sex with other guys.

A relationship with so little trust between the partners appears to be in trouble.

Lots of Options

Do you and your partner want to delay her next pregnancy? Plan now how you'll do so. There are a wide variety of contraceptives. Look at what's available. Then decide which is best for both of you.

You and your partner don't need a prescription for some contraceptives. You can buy these in almost any drugstore. These include:

- condom (rubber)
- spermicidal jelly or foam

All of these kill sperm or help keep them out of the uterus.

The condom helps prevent the spread of STIs (sexually transmitted infections).

STIs (Sexually Transmitted Infections): *Illness spread through sexual intercourse.*

The man needs to put the condom on carefully. He does this before his penis touches his partner's genitals. He rolls the condom on his erect penis. He should leave one-half inch of space at the end of the condom. This will make it feel more comfortable. It will also be less likely to break.

Remember, if you use a condom correctly and she uses foam, the two methods together are about as successful at preventing conception as is the pill or the IUD. Both the condom and foam can be bought at a drugstore with no prescription from the doctor.

Spermicide: *Product that kills sperm.*

The woman can use foam or jelly (spermicide) right before she has sex. She puts it in her vagina with a special little tool. Used alone, foam or jelly is *not* a reliable method of preventing pregnancy.

Foam or jelly work best when the man uses a condom.

Your local health department may provide the condom, foam, and jelly at no charge.

Teen Fathers Comment on Condoms

One young man, when asked if the man should be responsible for birth control, replied, "No, it's the mother's responsibility. I don't like to use condoms. I'll rely on my partner."

Other young fathers quoted in this book reacted strongly and negatively to his statement:

Tony, 16: *I'd recommend he use condoms. That's true – condoms don't feel right, but it doesn't matter whether it feels right or not. You should still use them.*

Agie, 18: *If you don't like the way it feels, I guess you're taking a chance to get a disease or to get a baby. It takes everything to raise a baby. If he's going to get together like that, go ahead if you want a baby or a disease.*

Jamal, 16: *That's a person who wants to catch AIDS or other STIs. At first I thought that about condoms, but when I see something that will harm me, I try to stop it. And unprotected sex is very, very harmful.*

Luis, 20: *That's stupid, not using a condom. You both should take precautions. You don't like the feel of the rubber, you can sit there and wait until you decide to use it.*

Don't count on withdrawal (pullout) to prevent pregnancy. (This means the man takes his penis out of the woman's body before he ejaculates.) Even sperm outside the vagina on the vulva can travel inside and cause pregnancy.

Withdrawal is not a reliable method of birth control. As a school nurse commented, "I've seen lots of cute little pullout babies!"

Birth Control Injections

Injectable medication, such as Depo-Provera, is a contraceptive alternative that differs from the other methods. The woman is given a shot which is 99 percent effective in preventing pregnancy for three months. Breastfeeding women can have the Depo-Provera injected at their six-week postpartum visit. For a non-breastfeeding mother, Depo-Provera can be injected as soon after birth as she wishes.

If your partner uses Depo-Provera, she needs to schedule an appointment with her healthcare provider every three months for her injection.

McKenna was using the Depo-Provera shot, but she was late getting her shot. The pregnancy was a big surprise. My mother set me down and made me understand there would be big changes in my life.
Saunders, 17 – Trilby, one year (McKenna, 16)

Birth Control Pill

Birth control pills for women are widely available from doctors and clinics. Insurance or Medicaid may pay for the pill. She doesn't have to take the pill right before having sex. That's an advantage. She does have to take one every day.

Is she breastfeeding the baby? Taking the pill might cut back on her supply of milk. If she's breastfeeding, she should talk to her doctor.

It might be best to choose another contraceptive until she weans baby to bottle or cup. Some pills, however, don't affect the making of breast milk.

Note: The pill will not prevent pregnancy the first month she takes it. Neither is the pill effective if she's taking antibiotics. If you have sex during that first month or while she's on antibiotics, use another contraceptive.

The pill will not protect either of you from STIs including AIDS.

Contraceptive Patch, Implant, IUD

The patch provides preventive hormones through the skin. It is a 11/2" x 11/2" patch. The woman places it on her skin and leaves it for 7 days. She repeats the process two times, then leaves it off while she has her period. Then she starts the process over again, using a new patch each time.

Another family planning device is the implant. It is a low dose of birth control medicine which the doctor puts under the skin of the woman's upper arm. It doesn't show. *Implanon* is a newer form of implant which may be more satisfactory.

Once there, the implant slowly releases the pregnancy-preventing medicine. This continues for three years. Some may prevent pregnancy for five years. Her insurance may cover the cost of the implant. If she wants the implant removed, her healthcare provider can do so.

The IUD (Intrauterine Device) for women is a plastic device about an inch long. It comes in various shapes.

The doctor places the IUD in the woman's uterus. Once there, it stays in for several years. The IUD is for women who have had a child. A woman using it should be having sex with only one man. With several partners, she would be more likely to get an infection from the IUD.

Other methods of birth control include the cervical cover, diaphragm, sponge, female condom, and the vaginal ring. If you and your partner are interested, see your healthcare provider.

Neither the IUD, Depo-Provera, the patch, nor the implant prevents the spread of STIs including AIDS. Only condoms can do that.

Emergency Contraception

If, in spite of good planning, unprotected sexual intercourse occurs, it is possible for the woman to see her healthcare provider for emergency contraception. There are medications that prevent pregnancy *if taken within 72 hours after intercourse*. They are 75 percent effective.

The emergency contraception pills have some mild side effects, but *much* less than pregnancy. The best plan is for you to use a condom and the woman to use another form of contraception *always*.

But don't despair if the unexpected occurs. For more information on emergency contraception, call 1.888.PREVEN2 (1.888.773.8362).

You and/or your partner might want to ask your healthcare provider for a prescription for emergency contraception so you'll have it on hand if necessary. Women over 18 can buy it without a prescription. In some states you can buy it online, <www.NOT-2-LATE.com>

STI Concerns

Sexually active people should be concerned about STIs. Some STIs are merely annoying, such as a yeast infection.

Others have serious and long-lasting effects. They need immediate treatment. AIDS is an STI that causes death.

Some STIs have obvious symptoms such as large sores on the skin. Others might not show anything on the outside at all. You can't be sure by looking at someone whether or not she has a disease.

Because of the diseases today, men should still wear condoms. They're a pain in a way, but it's either do you want to live or die any more.
Paul, 19 - Katherine, 4 months (Kyla, 15)

The best way not to get an STI is not to have sex. Next best is for the man to use a condom. It's safer if the woman uses a spermicidal jelly while the man uses a condom.

If you or your partner ever have any of these symptoms, see your doctor or go to a clinic:

- Painful urination (both men and women)
- Unusual discharge from the penis or vagina
- Sore or itching genitals
- Lumps or growths around genital areas
- Rashes or blisters on the genital area
- Sores on the penis, on the vulva, or in the vagina

Remember: Most STIs can be treated. Early treatment prevents serious lifelong effects. Medicaid and private insurance pay for this care. Public health departments provide free or very low cost treatment for STIs.

AIDS — An Incurable STI

AIDS cannot be treated successfully. AIDS stands for Acquired Immune Deficiency Syndrome.

The AIDS virus makes the body unable to fight diseases. A person with AIDS could die from any disease. Most often, cancer or pneumonia is the cause of death.

There are no early symptoms of AIDS. There is no cure. People who have AIDS are treated for their symptoms. However, they will not be cured.

In the past, some people got AIDS through blood transfusions. This is almost impossible today. Blood for transfusions is now thoroughly tested for the AIDS virus.

Today people get AIDS by:

- Having sex with an infected person.
- Sharing needles with infected people.
- Having sex with someone who shares needles with IV drug users.
- Being infected before or during birth by mother.

Caring for Yourself and Your Family

The more partners you have, the more likely you are to get an STI.

Things you can do to avoid STIs:

- Think about other ways to have a loving relationship.
- Protect both of you by using a condom during intercourse.
- Discuss protection from pregnancy before you begin sexual intercourse.
- Consider the risks of both pregnancy and STIs for you and your partner.

Planning for Your Next Child

Have your next child when you both are ready —

- physically
- emotionally
- financially

This will be better for your present child and for your future family.

She's on the pill and I use a condom. We don't push our luck — it's too easy to slip up. I think all my friends used to think they couldn't get a girl pregnant, and now they realize they have to be extra careful. Two of my friends have been together for a year, and they haven't slept together yet because we keep telling them it's not that important.

Heather was on the pill when she got pregnant, but she wasn't very responsible about taking it. Now every night I make sure she takes her pill before we go to bed. We don't want another baby right now.
Jason, 17 - Melanie, 13 months (Heather, 17)

If you and your partner don't want to be pregnant again, plan now to prevent it:

- Choose not to have sex, or
- If you're having intercourse, use birth control — always. The best protection against disease and unintended pregnancy is for each partner to use protection. Whatever method the woman uses, you should *always* use a condom to protect both of you against STIs.

The pregnancy prevention failure rate for condoms used alone is, for the first year, three percent with "perfect" use, and 14 percent with "typical" use. To protect both partners from unplanned pregnancy, the woman should also use a birth control method such as the pill, contraceptive implant, patch, or Depo-Provera.

Having your next child when you and your partner are physically, emotionally, and financially ready is better for your present child and your future family.

It's up to you and your partner to make this happen. And if your partner isn't interested, *it's up to you.*

A high school diploma and job training are important for dads.

16

Your Future — Your Child's Future

- **Looking ahead**
- **Your responsibilities as a father**
- **Establishing paternity**
- **Proving you're the father**
- **Taking financial responsibility**
- **Job helps self-esteem**
- **When you have other problems**
- **Finding community resources**
- **Don't give up**
- **Your long-range goals**

I had a job, but I lost it because business got slow. Once you lose that job, it's hard to find another one.

I was trying to make it in sports, a professional athlete, but Amy busted that dream.

I went back to school because I want to graduate. I want to be a fireman, and I think I can do that with six months of training.

Jermaine, 18 - Amy, 1
(Angela, 17)

Right now we have our own place. I work in a warehouse, and I'm part-time security. I was in school, but I had to drop out and start working. I'm trying to get back in school now.

Marco, 18 - Lily, 1 (Serene, 18)

Looking Ahead

What kind of future are you planning for you and for your child? If you're with his mother, are you developing a satisfying life together? Are you already an independent family, or on your way to becoming independent?

Are you spending lots of time with your child — touching, loving, and playing with him? Do you help care for him — feed him, change him, bathe him? These are all part of the "responsibility" thing. So is going with mom and baby to healthcare appointments. You just being there is important to your child. Being a dad is far more than making a baby.

If you aren't with your child's mother, are you still playing an important role in your child's life? Are you able to spend time with him regularly? Even if you don't live with him, he needs you.

Are you able to support your child? If you aren't to that point, what are you doing now to get there? Are you still in school? Are you learning job skills? It's essential that you be able to support yourself and your child.

Your Responsibilities as a Father

I see the babies with their moms and I wonder, "How can you have a kid in this world and not want it?" It's a part of you. I couldn't have my kid running around without me.

Jason, 17 - Melanie, 13 months (Heather, 17)

As a teenager, it's hard to "take your responsibilities" as a father, especially your financial responsibilities. If you haven't finished high school, finding a good job isn't easy.

Even if you have graduated, it won't be easy. The unemployment rate among teenage men is high.

If you're not working, people think you don't want to be responsible. If you've left school, they write you off as a typical teen father dropout. They think you will force your baby and his mother into a life of poverty.

Legally, you should provide for at least half of your child's support until she is 18. That's scary for a teenager with no job. Taking that responsibility at age 15 — or even 18 — may be impossible.

If you aren't yet 18, you may not be required to pay child support now. Laws vary from one state to another. However, many fathers, even with limited income, manage to provide some support for their child even as they continue their education and job training.

If you realize the cost of supporting a baby, you may feel like giving up. Many young fathers do. If they don't have money to pay for their baby's needs, they may give little or no help of any kind. Many others help as much as possible even as they continue their education and job training.

Establishing Paternity

If you aren't married to your child's mother, have you established paternity? It's important to do so for several reasons:

Identity: Your child needs to know who he is. There's a sense of belonging that comes from knowing both parents.

Benefits: Your child has a right to benefits from both parents. These may include Social Security, insurance benefits, inheritance rights, veterans' and other types of benefits. Unless you establish paternity, your child may not be able to claim these benefits through you.

Money: Both parents are required by law to support their child. A child who must rely on only one parent for financial support is likely not to have enough money for his needs.

Medical: Are there any health problems in your family? Your child needs to know.

If you aren't married to your child's mother, you establish legal paternity by affidavit, a legal paper that states you are the father of the child. Both you and your child's mother need to sign this affidavit. The actual procedure varies from state to state.

If you're the legal father, this gives you rights if the mother wants to place the child for adoption or if the authorities are trying to take the child away from the mother. You have no rights unless you have established legal paternity. If the state takes the child because the mother is on drugs, for example, you have no rights to your child if you haven't taken this step.

It's easier to establish paternity while you and the mother have a good relationship.

After she brought the baby home, her parents tried to keep me away from her. They would call the police. We weren't getting along, but now everything is working out okay.

If you're not married to your child's mother, it's important that you establish legal paternity. I went to a lawyer to learn about my rights. I also wanted to go down and establish visitation rights. Every man should know you sign the birth certificate, but you still need to go to the courthouse and she says under oath, "Yes, he's the father, I'm the mother." If there's disagreements, you have to get a blood test.

We plan on getting married, but I want to establish that I'm the father, and that I'll pay child support.

Some women think it's not necessary, but I feel every father should establish paternity. Then if the woman ever says, "I don't want you," it's done.
Paul, 19 - Katherine, 4 months (Kyla, 15)

Proving You're the Father

Is there any doubt that you're the father of your child? You can find out with nearly 100 percent accuracy through blood testing. This is a genetic test that compares many different factors in your blood with similar parts of the mother's and the child's blood.

If your child's mother marries someone else, you will still have rights and responsibilities toward your child. You'll still need to pay child support. Most important, you and your child will still have a right to know and to have a relationship with each other. You should be able to have visitation rights. Your child deserves both a mother and a father.

Ricardo is going to get hooked on to thinking that Lourdes' boyfriend is his father. I tell Lourdes there's going to be a time they'll have to tell Ricardo that's not his real father. I want Ricardo to grow up knowing I'm his real father.

I thought about forgetting about the baby because I have a lot of family problems, but I can't do that. He's something I created. A father should be there for his kid whether or not it was a mistake.
Angel, 18 - Ricardo, 3 months (Lourdes, 19)

It's best to establish paternity as early as possible. If you wait, things may change and you might not have a chance to assume responsibility for your child. She might grow up without knowing you and without the benefits that come from having both parents share in parental responsibilities. You can help give your baby the best possible chance in life by getting paternity established as soon as possible after she's born.

If you and your baby's mother don't live together, who does your baby live with? While mom is more likely to have day-to-day custody, you may have as much right to custody as mom does. Or you and baby's mom might share custody.

Taking Financial Responsibility

Julio had a low-paying job and, like many young fathers, wondered how he could possibly support his family:

> *I was working a construction job, making just a little over minimum wage. I thought, "Here we are, bringing a child into the world, and I'm going to have to support the child." I told the construction crew I was going to be a dad, and I wanted some advice.*
>
> *"Leave now," they told me.*
>
> *And "Get an abortion."*
>
> *I hung in there, and when Francene was born, we had benefits so the medical bills were paid. But so much else was on my mind. Will I be able to afford food? The bills? The responsibilities never end.*
>
> *I was worried about being a father. How do you fill a father's shoes, someone who's supposed to have all the answers? How do you live up to a father's reputation?*
>
> Julio, 24 - Francene, 4; Alina, 3; Gloria, 1 (Joanne, 22)

Whether you're the father or the mother, you need to live up to a parenting "reputation," as Julio says. You'll never have all the answers — none of us do — but you'll need to be responsible for your child. Being responsible includes being financially responsible as well as providing the companionship, love, and emotional support your child needs from you.

Job Helps Self-Esteem

I was working when my girlfriend was pregnant, but I quit for no reason. I just didn't like the job. Then it was hard to get a job because I didn't have any education. I was just doing little side jobs like helping friends fix cars.

Now I'm going to a program where they train us to get our GED and also train us in construction. We're building a two-story house now, basically for low-income people. Once I get through the program and graduate, sometime next year, they'll help me find a job.

Isaac, 18 – Brooke, 9 months (Alexis, 17)

A job can make a big difference in the way you feel about yourself. When you think well of yourself, when you have good self-esteem, you're a better father than when you're unhappy with yourself. Even if you're out of high school, you may need more job training.

Check community college catalogs for job training facilities. Possibilities may include Regional Occupation Programs (ROP) and high school career centers.

Also check for programs in your community that are funded by JTPA (Job Training Partnership Act). Your local Department of Social Services office could provide information.

I'll graduate a year from now. Right now I'm taking an ROP class — auto mechanics. If I don't get a job, I'll go to special training. They will teach me everything about a car, and it's free to ROP students. You learn six hours a day for a year plus you work part-time. Then they help you get a job.

I want always to be able to get a job, and auto mechanics will do that.

Raul, 16 - Marijo, 10 months (Sandra, 17)

As you plan your future, it's important that you plan how you'll earn enough money to support your child.

I thought the baby was going to be small forever. Soon she'll be a year old, and I still have a year of high school. I hope I can take her to the college childcare center while I get some training. I want to work with the phone company fixing the lines.

Damon, 16 - Samantha, 8 months (Roxanne, 15)

Even if the two parents are together and both are working, they may have heavy financial problems. Money seldom stretches as far as they'd like. The couple may not agree on how to spend the money they have:

Kyla doesn't understand that money isn't like water. You have to work for it. It's tough.

She doesn't see the difference between needing something and wanting something. If we can't have what we want now, maybe we can in the future, but it takes time. This causes a lot of fights.

Paul

Perhaps you and your partner could use some help in money management. You could probably find a class on this topic at your adult school. This might help you get the most benefit possible from the money you earn.

When You Have Other Problems

Of course not all problems come with dollar signs. Teen parents, like everyone else, have ups and downs in their lives. You may already be in school, or you may have a job. You may be making plans for your future and for your child's future.

If, however, your life is not going the way you want it to go, have you considered getting extra help? You don't have to handle everything by yourself. If you're having more problems than you can solve by yourself, the first step is to accept the fact that you need help. Some people find it very hard to admit they aren't making it on their own.

You're probably already getting informal help. Families often are a good source of support. So are friends. In fact, other young parents can offer tremendous support simply because they're facing some of the same problems that are bothering you. Daric joined a group for teen fathers at his school. It helped:

> *A lot of times I feel like I can't make it any more. I need support, and I don't get it at home. I get support in the group. It helps a lot knowing I'm not the only one in this situation. It makes me feel a lot better.*
>
> Daric, 16 - Kianna, 1 year (Kim, 18)

Is there a group at your school or in your community for teen fathers? If not, perhaps you could talk to a counselor, a teacher, or youth leader, and get such a group started.

Finding Community Resources

You may need help beyond what your family and friends can give. Perhaps they can suggest community resources for you to contact. Inquire about resources from other people with whom you interact — the director of a child-care center, your minister, doctor, or teacher. Check with your YMCA, youth clinic, and other local youth resources.

Also look in your telephone book. Your county or state Mental Health Association and Psychology Department at your local college may recommend counseling services.

If you or your partner is receiving financial assistance from Social Services, ask to see a social worker when you need special help. Social workers often have far too heavy case loads, but some are able to provide extra help to their clients. If you have a local community center, the social worker there may be able to tell you where to go for help with your problems. Your hospital social service department may be a good resource.

More than 300 agencies in the United States are connected with the Family Service Association of America. These agencies offer individual and family counseling at low cost, as well as a variety of other family services.

For the agency in your area, check your telephone directory under the following listings: Family Service Association, Council for Community Services, County Department of Health, Counseling Clinic, Mental Health Clinic, or United Way.

Don't Give Up

Generally you can get a list of hot lines from your telephone operator. Dial "411," then say, "I have this type of problem. Can you help me?"

You may find, as you call hot lines and other community services, that phone numbers you have been given are not helping you. Too often the number has been changed, your call is answered by a recording, or the person responding tells you that agency can't help you.

When this happens, don't give up. If a person answers your call but can't help, ask for referrals. Tell him/her you need help. You don't know where to call next. Explain how much you would appreciate any ideas s/he may give you.

Marriage and family counselors are usually listed in the telephone yellow pages. Your area may have a cost-free counseling agency, or the cost may be based on income. If you have very little income, you may not be charged a fee.

Independence and self-sufficiency are wonderful things — if they work. All of us need extra help at some time in our lives. If this is your time of special need, do whatever is necessary to get that help. Both you and your child will be glad you did. You and your child deserve the best there is. If you get your education and improve your vocational skills, you can be in charge of your life.

Your Long-Range Goals

Long-range goals are important, too. You may have long range plans for your child as Andy does:

> *I want Gus to grow good. I don't want him to be in the streets or nothing. I'm going to try to teach him what's right and what's wrong. I don't want him to grow up like I did or like my brothers.*
>
> Andy, 17 - Gus, 5 months (Yolanda, 15)

Andy's goal is fine, but the important thing is, what is he doing now to work toward that goal? Does it mean moving to a different neighborhood? Taking parenting classes? Improving his relationship with his child's mother?

Whatever your situation is, look at your goals for your child, then plan how to accomplish those goals.

Long-range goals are important for you, too. Where do you want to be in five years? What do you want to be doing? What kind of job will you have?

The problem with long-range goals, however, is that sometimes they may seem too easy. You may say, "In five years, I'll have a college degree and a well-paying job. We'll be married, have another baby, and a house."

That's a long-range goal, and if this is what you want, by all means continue planning and working toward it.

Most important, what are you doing this year, this month to work toward the life you want for yourself and your child? What must you do in order to continue your education? What steps can you take now to begin or continue your job skills training?

*What are you doing **today** to make a satisfying future for yourself and your child?*

About the Author

Jeanne Warren Lindsay is the author of twenty-one books for and about pregnant and parenting teens. More than 800,000 copies of her books had been sold by 2008. Her *Teen Dads: Rights, Responsibilities and Joys* was selected by the American Library Association as a Recommended Book for Reluctant Young Adult Readers.

Lindsay has worked with hundreds of pregnant and parenting teenagers. She developed the Teen Parent Program at Tracy High School, Cerritos, California, and coordinated the program for many years. Most of her books are written for pregnant and parenting teens, and quotes from interviewees are frequently used to illustrate concepts.

Lindsay grew up on a farm in Kansas. She has lived in the same house in Buena Park, California, for many years. She loves to visit the Middle West, but says she's now addicted to life in southern California. She has five grown children and seven grandchildren.

Lindsay is the editor of *PPT Express*, a quarterly newsletter for teachers and others working with pregnant and parenting teens. She speaks frequently at conferences across the country, and holds training sessions in her home for teen parent teachers. She says she's happiest while interviewing young people for her books or writing under the big avocado tree in her backyard.

Bibliography

The following bibliography contains books and a website of interest to young parents. Prices are quoted for the resources, but because prices change so rapidly, call your local or Internet book store for an updated price before ordering a book.

Allen, Nancy Kelly. ***Read to Me! I Will Listen: Tips Mom and Dad Can Use to Help Me Become a Lifelong Reader*** by Nancy Kelly Allen. $2.95, 10/$25, 25/$50; 100/$150. Morning Glory Press.
Child's view of the importance of parent reading to child.

Lansky, Vicki. ***Games Babies Play from Birth to Twelve Months.*** 2001. 100 pp. $10.95. Book Peddlers.
Many ideas for helping parents interact with their children in creative ways.

Leach, Penelope. ***Your Baby and Child from Birth to Age Five.*** Revised, 1997. 560 pp. $20. Alfred A. Knopf.
An absolutely beautiful book packed with information, many color photos and lovely drawings. Comprehensive, authoritative, and outstandingly sensitive guide to child care and development.

Lindsay, Jeanne Warren. ***Do I Have a Daddy? A Story About a Single-Parent Child.*** 2000. 48 pp. Paper, $7.95. Free study guide. Morning Glory Press.
A beautiful full-color picture book for the child who has never met his/her father. A special sixteen-page section offers suggestions to single mothers.

______. ***The P.A.R.E.N.T. Approach: How to Teach Young Moms and Dads the Art and Skills of Parenting*** by Lindsay. $12.95. Morning Glory Press.

Guide for social workers, home visitors, nurses, teachers working with teen parents.

Marecek, Mary. ***Breaking Free from Partner Abuse.*** 1999. 96 pp. $8.95. Quantity discount. Morning Glory Press.

Lovely edition illustrated by Jami Moffett. Underlying message is that the reader does not deserve to be hit. Simply written. Can help a young woman escape an abusive relationship.

MELD Parenting Materials. ***The New Middle of the Night Book: Answers to Young Parents' Questions When No One Is Around.*** 1999. 163 pp. $12.50. MELD, Suite 507, 123 North Third Street, Minneapolis, MN 55401.

Includes clearly written information about parenting during the first two years of life.

Morris, Jon. ***ROAD to Fatherhood: How to Help Young Dads Become Loving and Responsible Parents*** by Jon Morris. $14.95. Morning Glory Press.

Along with teen fathers' real stories, the book is a guide for teachers, counselors, social workers developing comprehensive services for young fathers.

Pantley, Elizabeth. ***The No-Cry Sleep Solution: Gentle Ways to Help Your Baby Sleep Through the Night.*** 2002. 108 pp. $15.95. Also ***The No-Cry Sleep Solution for Toddlers and Preschoolers.*** McGraw-Hill.

Both books offer positive approaches to help babies and toddlers get to bed, stay in bed, and sleep through the night.

Paschal, Angelia M. ***Voices of African-American Teen Fathers: I'm Doing What I Got to Do.*** 2006. 228 pp. Routledge. $39.95.

This examination of the lives of young African-American fathers shows a real mix of attitudes, misconceptions, expectations, and challenges.

Pollock, Sudie. ***Will the Dollars Stretch? Teen Parents Living on Their Own.*** 2001. 112 pp. $7.95. Teacher's Guide, $2.50. Morning Glory.

Five short stories about teen parents moving out on their own. As students read, they will get the feel of poverty as experienced by many teen parents — as they write checks and balance checkbooks of young parents involved.

_______. ***Moving On: Finding Information You Need for Living on Your Own.*** 2001. 48 pp. $4.95. 25/$75. Morning Glory Press.

Fill-in guide to help young persons find information about their community, information needed for living away from parents.

Pruett, Kyle. ***Fatherneed: Why Father Care Is as Essential as Mother Care for Your Child.*** 2001. 256 pp. Broadway. $19.

Author shows how infants are prewired for attachment to both men and women, and explains the lifelong benefits of this mutually beneficial relationship.

Reynolds, Marilyn. **True-to-Life Series from Hamilton High:** ***No More Sad Goodbyes. Shut Up! Baby Help. Beyond Dreams. But What About Me? Detour for Emmy. Telling. Too Soon for Jeff. Love Rules. If You Loved Me.*** 1993-2008. 160-256 pp. $8.95-$9.95. Morning Glory Press.
Wonderfully gripping stories about real situations faced by teens. Start with ***Too Soon for Jeff,*** *award-winning novel about a reluctant teen father. Students who read one of Reynolds' novels usually ask for more.*

Seward, Angela. Illustrated by Donna Ferreiro. ***Goodnight, Daddy.*** 2001. 48 pp. Paper, $7.95; hardcover, $14.95. Morning Glory Press.
Beautiful full-color picture book shows Phoebe's excitement because of her father's visit today. She is devastated when he calls to say, "Something has come up." Book illustrates the importance of father in the life of his child.

Silberg, Jackie. ***Games to Play with Babies.*** 2001. 256 pp. $14.95. ***Games to Play with Toddlers.*** 2002. 256 pp. $14.95. Gryphon.
Activities and games that don't require a lot of props.

Strand, Robert. ***The Power of Fatherhood.*** 2002. 96 pp. Evergreen Press. $5.99.
Easy-to-read book that encourages men to take their rightful place as fathers.

Teens Parenting Series: Your Pregnancy and Newborn Journey by Jeanne Warren Lindsay and Jean Brunelli PHN; ***Nurturing Your Newborn*** by Lindsay and Brunelli; ***Your Baby's First Year*** by Lindsay; ***Challenge of Toddlers*** by Lindsay; ***Discipline from Birth to Three*** by Lindsay and Sally McCullough; ***Mommy, I'm Hungry!*** by Lindsay, Brunelli, and McCullough; ***Teen Dads*** by Lindsay. First six titles are available in Spanish. Workbooks, teacher guides, and ***Comprehensive Curriculum Notebooks.*** Books, $12.95 ea. (***Nurturing Your Newborn,*** $7.95); Workbooks, $2.50 ea. Answer Keys, $4.95 ea. ***Comprehensive Curriculum Notebooks,*** $125 ea. Quantity discounts. Morning Glory Press.
Complete parenting curriculum designed especially for teenage parents. Lots of quotes from and photos of teen parents. Focuses on special needs of very young parents.

Wiggins, Pamela K. ***Why Should I Nurse My Baby?*** 1998. 58 pp. $5.95. Noodle Soup, 4614 Prospect Avenue, #328, Cleveland, OH 44103. 216.881.5151.
Easy-to-read, yet thorough discussion of breastfeeding. Question and answer format. Also ask about the ***Babies First*** *pamphlets, same source.*

Website: mypyramid.gov – U.S. Department of Agriculture. Put in your age, sex, and activity level, and you'll get a chart showing the foods *you* need. Do the same for your child 2 years or older.

DVDs — Sources, Representative Titles

(Contact distributors for current listings.)

Discipline from Birth to Three. Four DVDs, **Infants and Discipline — Meeting Baby's Needs, He's Crawling — Help!** (6-12 months), **She's into Everything!** (1-2 years), and **Your Busy Runabout** (2-3 years). 2001. 15 min. each. $195 set, $69.95 each. Morning Glory Press.

Wonderful videos over book of same title. Shows teens talking to teens, sharing techniques for loving care.

Life Skills for Teen Parents. 2007. Two volume set, $349.95. 35 min. ea. Injoy Videos.

Realistic, down-to-earth series gives teens concrete suggestions for moving forward in their lives.

Reading with Babies. Directed by Susan Straub. 2006. $25.00. The Read to Me Program, Inc. POB 730 Planetarium Station, New York, NY 10024-0539. **<www.readtomeprogram.org>**

Wonderful video that shows babies 0-24 months "reading" books with their parent(s) according to their developmental capacities. Realistic, playful portrayal of babies interacting with books.

Teen Breastfeeding: The Natural Choice. 20 min. **Teen Breastfeeding: Starting Out Right.** 35 min. Both for $139.95. Injoy Videos.

Wonderful videos. Part 1 provides reasons to breastfeed, and Part 2 tells how. Several teen moms star.

Too Soon for Jeff. 1996. 40 min. $89.95. Films for the Humanities and Sciences, P.O. Box 2053, Princeton, NJ 08543. 800.257.5126.

ABC After-School TV Special about reluctant teen father was based on the award-winning novel by Marilyn Reynolds and stars Freddie Prinze, Jr.

Your Baby's First Year. 2001. Four DVDs. **Nurturing Your Newborn, She's Much More Active** (4-8 months), **Leaving Baby Stage Behind, Keeping Baby Healthy.** 12-16 min. each. $195 set; $69.95 each. Morning Glory Press.

Teens talking to teens, sharing techniques for loving care. Based on book with same title. Includes teacher's guide with questions, projects, quiz.

Index